100 HEALTHY RECIPES

Healing
Soups

DELICIOUS RECIPES FOR BODY AND MIND

100 HEALTHY RECIPES

Healing Soups

DELICIOUS RECIPES FOR BODY AND MIND

BB Bounty
Books

Healing Soups

An Hachette UK Company
www.hachette.co.uk

Published in 2017 by Bounty Books,
a division of Octopus Publishing Group Ltd
Carmelite House
50 Victoria Embankment
London, EC4Y 0DZ
www.octopusbooks.co.uk

ISBN: 978-0-753732-15-1

A CIP catalogue record for this book is available
from the British Library

Printed and bound in China

10 9 8 7 6 5 4 3 2 1

Publisher: Lucy Pessell
Editor: Sarah Vaughan
Project Editor: Jane Birch
Production Controller: Beata Kibil
Designer: Chris Bell/cbdesign

Contents

introduction

Nourishing, easy to make and affordable, soup is endlessly adaptable, offering a host of benefits for all aspects of wellbeing. As renowned French chef Auguste Escoffier summed it up, 'Soup puts the heart at ease, calms down the violence of hunger, eliminates the tension of the day, and awakens and refines the appetite.'

Nutritional experts urge us to eat more health-boosting vegetables and a bowl of soup is an excellent way to do just that, giving you a good mix of minerals, nutrients and phytonutrients, the antioxidants found in plants that destroy harmful chemicals in your body.

Making your own ensures that you are getting the benefit of fresh ingredients while, at the same time, avoiding the additives and high sodium content of many commercially prepared soups. Homemade soup is wonderfully wholesome, as long as you go easy on the salt and saturated fat. Unlike other methods for cooking, soup retains the vitamins and minerals of cooked vegetables because you don't dispose of the vitamin-packed water when the veg is cooked; instead it become part of the delicious broth.

The healing soups in this book are targeted at different aspects of health and wellbeing so, whether you want something for a specific ailment or an all-round health booster, you'll be able to find the healing soup you need.

SOUP-MAKING EQUIPMENT

You don't need much specialist equipment for soup-making, but there are a few things that will help to ensure success:

Soup pot Opt for a large pot – one that is big enough for all the ingredients and that allows them to cook with space around them. Cheap, flimsy pots are a false economy; instead choose a solid pot with a heavy base, to prevent ingredients at the bottom from scorching during long cooking, and with two short handles that make it easy to grip the pot when lifting it. A pot that is higher than it's wide prevents too much liquid from evaporating.

Blender You can use this to process batches of soup quickly. For safety, allow the soup to cool a little before adding it the blender, make sure the lid is firmly on and blend in batches.

Hand blender Also called an immersion blender, a hand blender is a great soup-making tool as you avoid the potentially messy job of transferring the soup to the blender. It will make beautifully smooth puréed soup and it is easy to use and to clean.

Food processor You can use this both to purée soup and to prepare the vegetables.

CHOOSING INGREDIENTS

To get maximum health benefits from your soups, always buy fruit, vegetables and herbs in the best, freshest condition possible. Try to buy local produce that is in season. Chicken and meat should ideally be free-range and, if you can afford it, organic.

FINISHING TOUCHES

Turn your bowl of soup into a thing of beauty and add texture and interest with any of these healthy finishing touches:

Yogurt Swirl natural yogurt in a bowl of smooth-textured soup or add a spoonful of thick Greek yogurt or crème fraîche to the centre, perhaps with a few fresh herbs snipped over.

Seeds and nuts Sprinkle over crunchy pumpkin or sunflower seeds or a few flaked or roughly chopped nuts.

Herbs A handful of delicious chopped herbs, including parsley, basil, coriander or mint, will liven up any soup. For a topping with punch, try a sprinkling of gremolata – a mix of chopped parsley, lemon rind and chopped garlic – or salsa verde, which is a mix of chopped green herbs, anchovies, garlic and olive oil.

Oil A drizzle of good quality extra-virgin olive oil is delicious and looks elegant. You can also make your own herb-infused oils for drizzling.

Fruit and vegetable garnishes For a pretty garnish, try fine slices or shreds of apple, cucumber, carrot or pepper or tiny curls of lemon, lime or orange rind.

Spices A dusting of freshly grated nutmeg, a few crushed, dried chillies or a little paprika will add colour and depth of flavour. You could also try grated ginger, some roughly crushed peppercorns or, for a bright note, a light sprinkling of turmeric.

Croûtons Make a healthy version of this favourite soup topper by spraying cubes of wholegrain bread with a little olive oil, then bake in the oven until lightly golden.

STOCK

The best soups are those made from homemade stock. As part of the battle against food waste, it makes sense to get the most from the carcass of Sunday's roast chicken or to use up the slightly wrinkly carrots you found in the fridge. That said, sometimes there simply isn't time to make your own stock and supermarkets offer a whole range of prepared stock and bouillon cubes, powdered stock and chilled ready-made stocks. Some can be very strong in flavour so look out for ones that have reduced salt and make them up with a little extra water so that the flavour is not overpowering.

FISH STOCK

MAKES 3 litres (5 pints)

2 kg (4 lb) fish trimmings
1 tablespoon olive oil
1 fennel bulb, roughly chopped
1 carrot, roughly chopped
3 celery sticks, roughly chopped
6 garlic cloves, roughly chopped
250 ml (8 fl oz) white wine
3 litres (5 pints) cold water
juice of 1 lemon
2 bay leaves
1 lemon thyme sprig
handful of parsley

Remove the gills and eyes from any fish heads, if using, and wash all the bones thoroughly. Heat the oil in a large stockpot and sweat the vegetables and garlic, covered, for 5–6 minutes. Add the fish bones and trimmings and cook for a further 5 minutes.

Add the white wine, measurement water and lemon juice and bring to the boil. Reduce the heat to a simmer, add the herbs and simmer gently for 20–30 minutes, skimming when necessary.

Strain the stock then let it cool to room temperature. If you want to reduce the stock and intensify the flavour, simmer it gently until reduced by half, then allow to cool. Cover and refrigerate or freeze until required.

CHICKEN STOCK

MAKES 4 litres (7 pints)

2–2½ kg (4–5 lb) chicken carcasses
2 onions, chopped
1 garlic bulb, chopped
3 large carrots, trimmed
3 leeks, chopped
5 celery sticks, chopped
1 lemon, halved
handful of flat leaf parsley
4 bay leaves
2 rosemary sprigs
1 teaspoon black peppercorns
6 litres (10 pints) water

Put all the ingredients into a large stockpot and bring slowly to the boil. Reduce the heat to a simmer and cook, covered, for 2 hours.

Remove the lid and simmer the stock for at least 1 more hour until it is a rich golden colour and the bones are clean, skimming as necessary.

Strain the stock, let it cool to room temperature, then cover and refrigerate or freeze until required.

BEEF STOCK

5 kg (10 lb) beef bones and off-cuts
2 carrots, trimmed
4 onions, quartered
2 parsnips, trimmed
4 celery sticks, roughly chopped
1 leek, roughly chopped
1 garlic bulb, crushed
6 litres (10 pints) water
handful of parsley
2 bay leaves
2 teaspoons black peppercorns

MAKES 3 litres (5 pints)

Put the bones and meat into a large roasting tin, place in a preheated oven, 230°C (450°F), Gas Mark 8, and roast for 1 hour, turning regularly. Add the carrots, onions, parsnips, celery, leek and garlic and roast for 20 minutes, making sure they don't burn.

Transfer the bones, meat and vegetables to a large stockpot and cover with most of the measurement water. Deglaze the roasting tin over a medium heat with the remaining water then pour into the stockpot. Add the herbs and peppercorns and bring slowly to the boil, reduce the heat and simmer, covered, for 2 hours. Remove the lid, then simmer the stock for another 3–4 hours. Skim off the fat when necessary.

Strain the stock, let it cool to room temperature, then cover and refrigerate or freeze until required.

VEGETABLE STOCK

1 tablespoon olive oil
5 carrots, finely chopped
2 celery sticks with leaves, finely
   chopped
2 onions, finely chopped
2 leeks, finely sliced
1 fennel bulb, chopped
1 garlic bulb, unpeeled and roughly
   chopped
1 thyme sprig
1 rosemary sprig
1 bay leaf
handful of parsley
small bunch of basil
4 litres (7 pints) water
1 teaspoon sea salt
1 teaspoon black peppercorns

MAKES 4 litres (7 pints)

Heat the oil in a large stockpot and sweat all the vegetables and the garlic for 5–6 minutes.

Add the herbs, water, sea salt and peppercorns and bring to the boil, then lower the heat and simmer for 1½–2 hours, skimming occasionally.

Strain the stock through a sieve and let it cool.

SOUPS FOR LOOKING GOOD AND FEELING GOOD

introduction

'You are what you eat' is entirely true. Everything you eat becomes a part of how you look and feel, inside and out. Healthy food, including nourishing soups, means brighter skin and eyes and shiny hair, while your brain and your body, from your muscles to your heart, will be able to function better.

Soup is the ideal choice for keeping your body at a healthy weight or if you want to lose a few pounds. Several studies have found that soup can make you feel fuller for longer, and research has shown that regular soup eaters have healthier body mass indexes (BMI). And, as it has a high water content, it is ideal for those times when you've overdone it and want to detox.

From carrots to fight macular degeneration to fish for boosting brain power and heart-healthy soya beans to anti-ageing avocado, the soups in this chapter focus on providing the nourishment you need to make you feel and look great.

chunky spiced bean soup

SERVES 4
Prep + cook time: 35 minutes

2 tablespoons vegetable or olive oil
1 large onion, chopped
1 red pepper, cored, deseeded and chopped
1 red chilli, deseeded and finely chopped
2 cloves garlic, chopped (optional)
400 g (13 oz) can mixed beans or red kidney beans, rinsed and drained
500 g (1 lb) passata or sieved tomatoes
750 ml (1¼ pints) hot vegetable stock (see page 9 for homemade)
200 g (7 oz) mixed chopped frozen or leftover vegetables
salt and pepper
roughly chopped parsley, to garnish (optional)

Heat the oil in a large saucepan and add the onion, pepper, chilli and garlic, if using. Cook gently over a medium heat for 6–7 minutes until softened. Stir in the beans, passata and stock and bring to the boil. Reduce the heat slightly and simmer gently for 12–15 minutes until thickened slightly.

Add the vegetables and simmer gently for a further 3–4 minutes until just tender. Season to taste.

Ladle into bowls and serve hot, sprinkled with roughly chopped parsley, if desired.

Beans contain magnesium which helps relax the body to let it rest and restore energy. Magnesium also aids nerve function and blood pressure regulation.

chickpea & red pepper soup

SERVES 4
Prep + cook time: 30 minutes

2 tablespoons olive oil
1 onion, finely chopped
1 red pepper, cored, deseeded
  and chopped
2 garlic cloves, crushed
2 teaspoons tomato purée
1 teaspoon ground cumin
½ teaspoon ground coriander
pinch of cayenne pepper
pinch of saffron threads
1.5 litres (2½ pints) hot vegetable
  stock (see page 9 for homemade)
400 g (13 oz) can chickpeas, rinsed
  and drained
125 g (4 oz) couscous
finely grated rind and juice of 1 lemon
salt and pepper
handful of chopped mint
handful of chopped fresh coriander

Heat the oil in a large saucepan. Add the onion and cook for 5 minutes, then add the red pepper, garlic, tomato purée and spices and cook for a further 1 minute.

Pour in the stock and bring to the boil, then reduce the heat and simmer for 5 minutes. Add the chickpeas and simmer for a further 5 minutes, then season to taste.

Add the couscous and a squeeze of lemon juice and cook for 1 minute until the couscous is tender.

Divide among bowls and sprinkle with the herbs and grated lemon rind before serving.

This colourful soup also contains red pepper, a great source of vitamin C to help in the proper absorption of iron, which is essential for energy.

Vietnamese beef pho

THE SCIENCE BIT

Beef is an excellent source of easily absorbed iron which is vital to fight fatigue. Beef also provides protein and vitamin B12.

SERVES 4
Prep + cook time: 20 minutes

1.5 litres (2½ pints) chicken stock
  (see page 8 for homemade)
2 lemon grass stalks, bruised
small piece of fresh root ginger,
  peeled and sliced
2 tablespoons light soy sauce
2 tablespoons lime juice
2 teaspoons soft brown sugar
125 g (4 oz) flat rice noodles
1 tablespoon sunflower oil
275 g (9 oz) sirloin steak
150 g (5 oz) bean sprouts
1 red chilli, thinly sliced
handful of Thai basil leaves
handful of mint

Place the stock, lemon grass, ginger, soy sauce, lime juice and sugar in a large saucepan, bring to the boil and simmer gently for 10 minutes.

Remove the lemon grass and ginger with a slotted spoon and add the noodles. Cook according to the packet instructions.

Meanwhile, heat the oil in a frying pan, add the steak and cook according to taste. Trim off the fat then cut into slices.

Ladle the pho into bowls immediately, top with steak slices, bean sprouts, chilli, basil and mint.

Pronounced 'fuh', pho is a noodle soup that originated in the northern city of Hanoi. It is a popular street food throughout Vietnam.

jerk chicken & sweet potato soup

SERVES 4–6

Prep + cook time: 30 minutes

2 tablespoons vegetable oil
1 red onion, chopped
1 celery stick, chopped
2.5 cm (1 inch) piece of fresh root
  ginger, peeled and chopped
1 tablespoon jerk seasoning
1 kg (2 lb) sweet potato, chopped
  (or use a mixture of sweet potato
  and butternut squash)
1.2 litres (2 pints) hot chicken stock
  (see page 8 for homemade)
2 tablespoons lime juice
250 g (8 oz) cooked chicken,
  shredded
salt and pepper
thinly sliced spring onions, to garnish

Heat the vegetable oil in a large saucepan and fry the onion, celery and ginger for 4–5 minutes, until beginning to soften. Add the jerk seasoning, then mix in the sweet potato and stir over the heat for 1 minute.

Pour the chicken stock into the pan and simmer over a medium heat for about 12 minutes, until the potato is tender. Blend to the desired consistency, then stir in the lime juice and season to taste.

Ladle the soup into bowls and top each with a handful of the shredded chicken. Garnish with spring onions and serve.

Staying hydrated is key to avoiding headaches and fatigue. Soup is great for keeping up hydration but you should also remember to drink plenty of water throughout the day.

pesto, pea & broccoli soup

THE SCIENCE BIT

Broccoli, tomatoes and potatoes are all excellent sources of vitamin C for radiant skin and to help heal blemishes.

SERVES 4
Prep + cook time: 30 minutes

2 tablespoons olive oil
1 onion, finely chopped
1 baking potato, about 275 g (9 oz), diced
1 garlic clove, chopped
200 g (7 oz) can tomatoes
900 ml (1½ pints) chicken or vegetable stock (see pages 8 and 9 for homemade)
175 g (6 oz) broccoli, cut into tiny florets and stalks sliced
125 g (4 oz) frozen peas
2 teaspoons ready-made pesto, plus extra to garnish
salt and pepper
a few basil leaves, to garnish
freshly grated Parmesan cheese, to serve

Heat the oil in a large saucepan, add the onion and fry for 5 minutes, until lightly browned. Add the potato and garlic and fry for 5 further minutes, stirring, until softened.

Add the tomatoes and stock, and season with salt and pepper, then bring to the boil. Cover the pan and simmer for 10 minutes, until reduced and thickened. Add the broccoli, peas and pesto and simmer for 3–4 minutes, until the broccoli is just tender.

Garnish the soup with a little extra pesto and the basil and serve with Parmesan.

Peas have anti-inflammatory properties that will help to reduce wrinkles and can help to soothe acne and blemishes naturally.

tomato risoni soup

THE SCIENCE BIT

Collagen is what gives skin its strength and structure. The synthesis of collagen relies on vitamin C which tomatoes have in abundance.

SERVES 4
Prep + cook time: 30 minutes

2 tablespoons olive oil, plus extra
    for drizzling
4 large tomatoes
1 large onion, finely chopped
2 celery sticks, finely chopped
1.5 litres (2½ pints) vegetable stock
    (see page 9 for homemade)
150 g (5 oz) dried risoni or orzo or
    any tiny shaped dried pasta
6 tablespoons finely chopped flat
    leaf parsley
salt and pepper

Heat the oil in a large saucepan over a medium heat, add the onion and celery and cook until soft.

Meanwhile, score a cross in the base of each tomato, then put in a heatproof bowl of boiling water for 1 minute. Plunge into cold water, then peel the skin away from the cross. Halve the tomatoes, then scoop out the seeds and discard. Roughly chop the flesh.

Add the tomatoes and stock to the pan and bring to the boil. Add the pasta and cook for 10 minutes or until al dente. Season to taste with salt and pepper and stir in the parsley.

Remove from the heat, ladle into bowls and drizzle with oil before serving.

Lycopene, found in tomatoes, can lower the risks of heart disease and some cancers. Research has shown that cooking tomatoes increases their lycopene levels.

Thai hot & sour prawn soup

THE SCIENCE BIT

Shellfish contains selenium, an antioxidant that research suggests can help protect the skin against sun damage and age spots.

SERVES 4

Prep + cook time: 10 minutes

1 tablespoon tom yum or Thai red
  curry paste
1.5 litres (2½ pints) hot chicken
  or fish stock (see page 8 for
  homemade)
2 cm (¾ inch) piece of fresh
  root ginger
1 lemon grass stalk
2 kaffir lime leaves
1 teaspoon brown sugar
1 tablespoon Thai fish sauce
400 g (13 oz) oyster mushrooms,
  sliced
250 g (8 oz) raw large prawns
lime juice, to taste
handful of chopped fresh coriander,
  to garnish

Heat a large saucepan. Add the curry paste, then stir in the stock, ginger, lemon grass, lime leaves, sugar and fish sauce. Bring to the boil, then reduce the heat and simmer for 5 minutes.

Add the mushrooms and prawns and season to taste. Cook for a further 3–4 minutes until the prawns are just cooked through. Add lime juice to taste.

Remove the ginger, lemon grass and lime leaves if liked, and serve immediately, scattered with the coriander.

Kaffir lime leaves have an intense citrus fragrance and are frequently used in southeast Asian recipes in much the same way as bay leaves are used in Western cooking.

sweet potato & coconut soup

SERVES 4

Prep + cook time: 45 minutes

2 tablespoons olive oil
1 onion, finely chopped
2 garlic cloves, crushed
1 teaspoon peeled and grated fresh
　root ginger
grated rind and juice of 1 lime
1 red chilli, deseeded and chopped
750 g (1½ lb) sweet potatoes,
　peeled and roughly chopped
600 ml (1 pint) vegetable stock
　(see page 9 for homemade)
400 g (13 oz) can coconut milk
150 g (5 oz) baby spinach leaves
salt and pepper

Heat the oil in a large saucepan, add the onion, garlic, ginger, lime rind and chilli and cook over a low heat, stirring frequently, for 5 minutes until the onion is softened. Add the sweet potatoes and cook, stirring frequently, for 5 minutes.

Stir in the stock, coconut milk, lime juice and salt and pepper. Bring to the boil, then reduce the heat, cover and simmer gently for 15 minutes, or until the potatoes are tender.

Transfer half the soup to a food processor or blender and process until smooth. Return to the pan, stir in the spinach and cook until just wilted. Adjust the seasoning and serve immediately.

This delicious Asian-inspired soup also contains ginger. Native to southeastern Asia, India and China, ginger has been valued for its culinary and medicinal properties for thousands of years.

tomato & basil soup

SERVES 4
Prep + cook time: 30 minutes

2 tablespoons olive or vegetable oil
1 large onion, chopped
2 garlic cloves, chopped
500 g (1 lb) passata
400 g (13 oz) can chickpeas, rinsed
  and drained
500 ml (17 fl oz) hot chicken or
  vegetable stock (see pages 8 and 9
  for homemade)
1 small bunch of basil, roughly
  chopped
salt and pepper

Heat the oil in a large saucepan and cook the onion over a medium heat for 7–8 minutes until softened. Add the garlic and cook gently for a further 2 minutes until softened.

Pour the passata and chickpeas into the pan with the hot stock, then bring to the boil and simmer gently for 15 minutes until rich and thickened slightly.

Add the basil leaves, reserving a few for garnish. Season to taste, then blend until smooth and thick, adding a little extra water for the desired consistency.

Ladle into bowls and serve garnished with the reserved basil leaves.

Staring at your computer screen for too long can make your eyes dry so make sure you look away from the screen every 20 minutes to give them a rest.

Jamaican spiced corn chowder

THE SCIENCE BIT

Corn is a great source of lutein and zeaxanthin to protect eyes. To maximize absorption, eat it together with a dietary fat such as olive oil.

SERVES 4

Prep + cook time: 30 minutes

1 tablespoon olive oil
1 large onion, finely chopped
2 garlic cloves, finely chopped
1 teaspoon cayenne pepper
200 g (7 oz) red split lentils, rinsed
1 litre (1¾ pints) hot vegetable
  stock (see page 9 for homemade)
400 ml (14 fl oz) can coconut milk
1 Scotch bonnet chilli, left whole
1 tablespoon thyme leaves
200 g (7 oz) potatoes, peeled and
  cut into 1 cm (½ in) dice
200 g (7 oz) carrots, peeled and cut
  into 1 cm (½ in) dice
400 g (13 oz) sweetcorn kernels
  (either fresh, frozen or canned)
2 red peppers, cored, deseeded and
  cut into 1 cm (½ in) dice
salt and pepper
chopped coriander, to garnish

Heat the oil in a large saucepan and stir-fry the onion and garlic for 2–3 minutes.

Increase the heat, add the cayenne pepper, red lentils, stock, coconut milk, chilli, thyme, potato and carrots. Bring to the boil and simmer for 15–20 minutes.

Season and add the corn and red pepper for the last 3 minutes of cooking.

Remove the Scotch bonnet chilli, ladle the chowder into bowls and serve garnished with chopped coriander and sprinkled with pepper.

A staple of Jamaican cooking, the Scotch bonnet chilli adds heat to this satisfying soup. Chillies contain capsaicin, a phytochemical that offers a host of healing benefits from fighting cancer to protecting against heart attacks and stroke.

caldo verde

SERVES 4

Prep + cook time: 50 minutes

125 g (4 oz) dark green cabbage,
  e.g. Cavolo Nero
4 tablespoons olive oil
1 large onion, chopped
625 g (1½ lb) floury potatoes, cut
  into small chunks
2 garlic cloves, chopped
1 litre (1¾ pints) vegetable stock
  (see page 9 for homemade)
400 g (13 oz) can cannellini beans,
  rinsed and drained
15 g (½ oz) fresh coriander,
  roughly chopped
salt and pepper

Discard any tough stalk ends from the cabbage and roll the leaves up tightly. Using a large knife, shred the cabbage as finely as possible.

Heat the oil in a large saucepan and gently fry the onion for 5 minutes. Add the potatoes and cook, stirring occasionally, for 10 minutes. Stir in the garlic and cook for a further 1 minute.

Add the stock and bring to the boil. Reduce the heat and simmer gently, covered, for about 10 minutes until the potatoes are tender. Use a potato masher to lightly mash the potatoes into the soup so that they are broken up but not completely puréed.

Stir in the beans, shredded cabbage and coriander and cook gently for a further 10 minutes. Season to taste with salt and pepper.

carrot & coriander soup

THE SCIENCE BIT

The old adage about carrots being good for eyesight is true – they really do help fight against macular degeneration.

SERVES 4

Prep + cook time: 30 minutes

1 tablespoon olive oil

2 bay leaves

1 onion, roughly chopped

2 garlic cloves, chopped

625 g (1¼ lb) carrots, roughly chopped

small bunch of coriander, leaves separated from stems

1.2 litres (2 pints) vegetable stock (see page 9 for homemade)

½ teaspoon garam masala

salt and pepper

4 tablespoons Greek yogurt, to garnish

Heat the oil in a large saucepan, add the bay leaves, onion and garlic and fry for 2 minutes. Add the carrots, coriander stems and stock and bring to the boil. Simmer until the carrots are completely cooked.

Let the soup cool slightly, remove the bay leaves and blend until smooth. If you like a very smooth soup, strain through a fine sieve. Reheat gently and season with salt, pepper and the garam masala. Finely chop half the coriander leaves and stir them into the soup.

Ladle the soup into bowls and garnish with a tablespoon of Greek yogurt and the remaining coriander leaves.

Used in many Indian dishes, garam masala is an aromatic blend of spices that typically includes peppercorns, cloves, cardamom and cinnamon.

chorizo & black bean soup

SERVES 4
Prep + cook time: 25 minutes

2 tablespoons vegetable oil
1 onion, finely chopped
125 g (4 oz) chorizo, finely diced
1 red pepper, cored, deseeded and
   chopped
1 garlic clove, chopped
1 teaspoon ground cumin
1.5 litres (2½ pints) hot chicken
   stock (see page 8 for homemade)
2 × 400 g (13 oz) cans black beans,
   rinsed and drained
salt and pepper
2 tablespoons lime juice
4 tablespoons soured cream
handful of chopped fresh coriander
   leaves
1 red chilli, chopped

Heat the oil in a large saucepan. Add the onion, chorizo, red pepper and garlic and cook for 7–10 minutes until soft, then stir in the cumin. Pour in the stock and beans and simmer for 5–8 minutes.

Season to taste, then use a potato masher to roughly mash some of the beans to thicken the soup.

Ladle the soup into bowls and squeeze a little lime juice over each portion. Add a spoonful of soured cream, top with a sprinkling of coriander and chilli and serve immediately.

Beans contain protein along with hair-friendly iron, zinc and biotin. Biotin encourages hair growth by strengthening the structure of the strands of hair.

spiced coconut & butternut squash soup

SERVES 4–6

Prep + cook time: 40 minutes

2 tablespoons oil

1 onion, chopped

2 teaspoons peeled and finely chopped fresh root ginger

½ teaspoon ground coriander

1 lemon grass stalk

1 strip of orange peel

1 kg (2 lb) butternut squash, peeled and chopped

1 litre (1¾ pints) vegetable stock (see page 9 for homemade)

125 ml (4 fl oz) coconut milk

salt and pepper

1 red chilli, deseeded and chopped and a handful of chopped fresh coriander, to serve

Heat the oil in a large saucepan, add the onion and cook for 5 minutes until softened. Add the ginger, ground coriander, lemon grass, orange peel and squash. Pour in the stock and coconut milk and bring to the boil. Leave to simmer for 12–15 minutes until the squash is soft.

Remove the lemon grass and orange peel and blend the soup until smooth. Season to taste.

Divide among bowls. Sprinkle over the chilli and fresh coriander before serving.

Ginger has been used for centuries in Ayurvedic treatments for hair. The ginger in this spicy, warming soup will boost blood circulation, encouraging new hair growth.

chicken mulligatawny

SERVES 6

Prep + cook time: 1 hour 50 minutes

50 g (2 oz) butter

600 g (1 lb 3 oz) bone-in, skinless chicken thighs

2 onions, chopped

2 small carrots, chopped

1 small cooking apple, peeled, cored and chopped

1 tablespoon plain flour

1 litre (1¾ pints) chicken stock (see page 8 for homemade)

2 tablespoons mild curry paste

2 tablespoons tomato purée

50 g (2 oz) basmati rice

natural yogurt, for topping

salt and pepper

Melt half the butter in a large saucepan and fry the chicken thighs in two batches for 5 minutes each, until golden on all sides. Lift out with a slotted spoon on to a plate. Add the remaining butter and fry the onions, carrots and apple, stirring, for 6–8 minutes until lightly browned.

Sprinkle in the flour and cook, stirring, for 1 minute. Gradually blend in the stock, then stir in the curry paste, tomato purée and rice. Return the chicken to the pan and bring to a simmer, stirring. Reduce the heat, cover and cook very gently for 1 hour until the chicken is cooked through and very tender.

Lift the chicken pieces from the pan. Once cool enough to handle, pull the meat from the bones. Shred half the meat into pieces and return the remainder to the pan. Blend the soup until smooth.

Return the shredded chicken to the pan and heat through. Season to taste with salt and pepper and serve topped with spoonfuls of natural yogurt.

haddock & spinach chowder

THE SCIENCE BIT

Experts recommend eating two portions of brain-building fish a week, while a diet that includes plenty of spinach can help keep your brain alert in old age.

SERVES 4

Prep + cook time: 35 minutes

50 g (2 oz) butter
1 tablespoon sunflower oil
1 large onion, chopped
1 large baking potato, diced
900 ml (1½ pints) semi-skimmed
   milk
1 fish stock cube
2 bay leaves
freshly grated nutmeg
400 g (13 oz) smoked haddock fillet,
   halved
125 g (4 oz) baby spinach leaves,
   stems removed and torn into
   pieces
salt and pepper
4 grilled rindless streaky bacon
   rashers, to garnish (optional)

Heat the butter and oil in a large saucepan, add the onion and fry gently for 5 minutes, until softened but not browned. Add the potato and fry for a further 5 minutes, stirring, until lightly browned.

Stir in the milk, stock cube, bay leaves, nutmeg and salt and pepper to taste. Add the haddock and bring to the boil, then cover the pan and simmer for 10 minutes until the haddock is cooked and flakes easily.

Lift the haddock out of the pan on to a plate, peel off the skin and flake the flesh into pieces, carefully removing any bones, then set aside. Add the spinach to the pan and cook for 2–3 minutes, until tender. Return the haddock to the pan and reheat.

Ladle the soup into bowls and garnish with the bacon, if using.

parsnip, sage & chestnut soup

THE SCIENCE BIT

For centuries sage has been thought to improve concentration and a 2003 study confirms that this common herb does indeed help concentration and memory.

SERVES 4
Prep + cook time: 1 hour

3 tablespoons chilli oil, plus extra
   for drizzling
40 sage leaves
1 leek, chopped
500 g (1 lb) parsnips, roughly
   chopped
1.2 litres (2 pints) vegetable stock
   (see page 9 for homemade)
pinch of ground cloves
200 g (7 oz) pack cooked peeled
   chestnuts
2 tablespoons lemon juice
crème fraîche, for topping
salt and pepper

Heat the chilli oil in a large saucepan until a sage leaf sizzles and crisps in 15–20 seconds and fry the remaining leaves in batches until crisp, lifting out with a slotted spoon onto a plate lined with kitchen paper. Set aside.

Add the leek and parsnips to the pan and fry gently for 10 minutes until softened. Add the stock and cloves and bring to the boil. Reduce the heat, cover and cook very gently for 30 minutes until the vegetables are very soft. Stir in the chestnuts and cook for a further 5 minutes.

Blend the soup until smooth. Add the lemon juice and reheat gently, seasoning to taste with salt and pepper.

Ladle into bowls, top with a little crème fraîche and drizzle sparingly with extra chilli oil. Serve scattered with the sage leaves.

tomato & chorizo soup

SERVES 4

Prep + cook time: 20 minutes

3 tablespoons olive oil

1 red onion, chopped

2 garlic cloves, chopped

1 teaspoon hot smoked paprika

2 x 400 g (13 oz) cans butter beans, rinsed and drained

100 g (3½ oz) sun-dried tomatoes, drained

500 g (1 lb) passata

900 ml (1½ pints) vegetable stock (see page 9 for homemade)

150 g (5 oz) chorizo, diced

salt and pepper

chopped parsley, to garnish

Heat 2 tablespoons of the oil in a large saucepan and cook the onion and garlic over a medium heat for 4–5 minutes, until slightly softened.

Add the paprika and butter beans and stir for 1 minute before adding the sun-dried tomatoes, passata and stock. Bring to the boil, then simmer for about 10 minutes, until thickened slightly.

Meanwhile, heat the remaining oil in a small frying pan and cook the chorizo for 2–3 minutes, stirring frequently, until golden. Drain on kitchen paper and set aside.

Blend the soup to the desired consistency, then season to taste and ladle into bowls. Top with the chorizo and parsley and serve immediately.

lamb & sweet potato soup

THE SCIENCE BIT

Ginger is a potent anti-inflammatory, the gingerols in it working against soreness in tired muscles and easing joint pain.

SERVES 6

Prep + cook time: around 3 hours
  15 minutes

1 tablespoon olive oil
500 g (1 lb) stewing lamb on the
  bone
1 onion, finely chopped
1–2 garlic cloves, finely chopped
2.5 cm (1 inch) piece of fresh root
  ginger, peeled and grated
2 teaspoons ras el hanout
  (Moroccan spice blend)
2 litres (3½ pints) lamb or chicken
  stock (see page 8 for homemade)
75 g (3 oz) red lentils, rinsed and
  drained
300 g (10 oz) sweet potatoes,
  peeled and diced
175 g (6 oz) carrots, diced
salt and pepper
small bunch of fresh coriander, to
  garnish (optional)

Heat the oil in a large saucepan over a medium-high heat. Add the lamb and fry for a couple of minutes until browned on one side. Reduce the heat slightly, turn the meat over and add the onion. Continue cooking until the lamb is browned all over and the onion is softened and starting to colour.

Stir in the garlic, ginger and ras el hanout. Cook, stirring, for about 30 seconds until fragrant, then add the stock and lentils. Season with salt and pepper. Bring to the boil, reduce the heat, cover and simmer for 1½ hours.

Add the sweet potatoes and carrots, bring back to a simmer, then cover the pan again and simmer the soup gently for 1 hour. Lift the lamb out of the soup with a slotted spoon, transfer to a plate and carefully remove the bones and any excess fat, breaking the meat into small pieces. Return the meat to the pan and heat through. Taste and adjust the seasoning if liked.

Ladle the soup into bowls and serve sprinkled with torn coriander leaves.

spiced pumpkin & spinach soup

THE SCIENCE BIT

Packed with vitamin A and beta-carotene, orange vegetables including sweet potatoes and pumpkin are strong inflammation fighters.

SERVES 4

Prep + cook time: 45 minutes

50 g (2 oz) butter

2 tablespoons olive oil

1 onion, roughly chopped

2 garlic cloves, peeled

1.5 kg (3 lb) pumpkin, peeled and
   roughly chopped

1 teaspoon ground coriander

½ teaspoon cayenne pepper

½ teaspoon ground cinnamon

¼ teaspoon ground allspice

750 ml (1¼ pints) hot vegetable
   stock (see page 9 for homemade)

150 g (5 oz) frozen spinach

salt and pepper

2 tablespoons lightly toasted
   pumpkin seeds and 4 teaspoons
   pumpkin seed oil, to serve

Heat the butter and oil in a large saucepan and add the onion and garlic. Cook over a medium heat for 5–6 minutes until soft and golden.

Add the pumpkin and continue cooking for a further 8 minutes, stirring frequently, until beginning to soften and turn golden. Add the spices and cook for 2–3 minutes, making sure that the pumpkin is well coated.

Pour in the hot stock and bring to the boil, then reduce the heat, cover and leave to bubble gently for about 15 minutes until the pumpkin is soft.

Blend the soup until smooth, then stir in the spinach. Reheat for about 5 minutes until the spinach has thawed and the soup is hot. Season to taste.

Spoon the soup into bowls, scatter over the lightly toasted pumpkin seeds and a drizzle of pumpkin oil and serve immediately.

savoy cabbage & parmesan soup

SERVES 4
Prep + cook time: 40 minutes

4 tablespoons olive oil
1 onion, chopped
2 garlic cloves, crushed
½ teaspoon fennel seeds
1 Savoy cabbage
1 potato, peeled and diced
1 litre (1¾ pints) vegetable stock (see page 9 for homemade)
75 g (3 oz) grated Parmesan cheese, plus extra 1 tablespoon to serve
salt and pepper

Heat 2 tablespoons of the olive oil in a saucepan and sauté the onion, garlic and fennel seeds for 3–4 minutes.

Shred 4 leaves of the cabbage and reserve. Finely shred the remaining cabbage, add to the pan with the diced potato and cook for 3–4 minutes, then pour in the stock. Simmer for 10 minutes, until the potato is tender. Stir in the grated Parmesan. Blend until smooth, then season to taste.

Heat the remaining olive oil and stir-fry the reserved cabbage.

Ladle the soup into bowls, top each bowl of soup with the fried cabbage and serve sprinkled with extra grated Parmesan.

Savoy cabbage contains copper to help build collagen to form cartilage and ligaments and is rich in sulforaphane, a compound that may block enzymes linked to joint inflammation.

light clam & tomato broth

SERVES 4

Prep + cook time: 30 minutes

150 g (5 oz) tomatoes
2 tablespoons olive oil
2 garlic cloves, finely chopped
150 ml (¼ pint) dry white wine
2 litres (3½ pints) hot chicken
   or fish stock (see page 8 for
   homemade)
5 sun-dried tomatoes in oil, drained
   and finely chopped
200 g (7 oz) anellini pasta
1 kg (2 lb) clams, cleaned
salt and pepper
chopped flat leaf parsley, to garnish
lemon wedges, to serve

Cut a cross at the stem end of each tomato, place in a heatproof bowl and pour over boiling water to cover. Leave for 1–2 minutes, then drain and peel off the skins. Halve the tomatoes, remove the seeds and roughly chop.

Heat the oil in a large saucepan, add the garlic and cook for 30 seconds until beginning to turn golden. Pour over the wine and cook for 5 minutes until slightly reduced. Pour over the stock and bring to the boil. Add the fresh and sun-dried tomatoes, season and simmer for 5 minutes.

Add the pasta and clams, cover with a lid and cook for 5 minutes until the pasta has cooked through and the clams have opened. Discard any that remain closed. Season to taste.

Ladle into bowls, sprinkle with the parsley and serve with lemon wedges.

creamy wild mushroom soup

SERVES 4
Prep + cook time: 35 minutes

375 g (12 oz) mixed fresh wild
    mushrooms, such as morels,
    shiitake and oyster
1 tablespoon olive oil
1 onion, roughly chopped
1 potato, finely diced
1 litre (1¾ pints) chicken stock
    (see page 8 for homemade)
2 garlic cloves, crushed
350 ml (12 fl oz) crème fraîche
salt and pepper

Chop the mushrooms very finely, reserving a few whole ones for the garnish. Put half the oil into a large saucepan and cook the onion and potato gently for 10 minutes, or until the onion is translucent and the potato cooked through. Transfer the mixture to a food processor or blender, cover with some of the stock and blend until smooth.

Put the chopped and whole mushrooms and garlic into the pan with the remaining oil and sweat gently for about 5 minutes. Add the remaining stock and bring to the boil; reduce heat and simmer for a few minutes. Remove the whole mushrooms and reserve.

Gently combine the potato mixture with the crème fraîche in a large bowl. Remove the soup from the heat and add a ladleful of hot stock to the crème fraîche mixture, stirring briskly. Add another couple of ladlefuls, and stir carefully.

Return everything to the pan and mix thoroughly. Replace the pan on a very low heat and reheat gently. Season to taste. Ladle into bowls and serve garnished with the reserved mushrooms.

Indonesian chicken & peanut soup

THE SCIENCE BIT

Peanuts contain the phytochemical resveratrol, which has been linked to a significant decrease in heart disease.

SERVES 4
Prep + cook time: 35 minutes

1 litre (1¾ pints) chicken stock
  (see page 8 for homemade)
2 tablespoons soy sauce
1½ tablespoons molasses
2 tablespoons lemon juice
2 garlic cloves
40 g (1½ oz) smooth peanut butter
50 g (2 oz) unsalted peanuts,
  chopped
125 g (4 oz) cooked chicken,
  shredded
75 g (3 oz) spring onions, finely
  sliced

Combine the stock, soy sauce, molasses, lemon juice and garlic in a large saucepan. Bring to the boil then reduce the heat and simmer, uncovered, for about 15 minutes.

Whisk in the peanut butter and simmer for 5 minutes.

When you are ready to serve, stir in the peanuts, chicken and spring onions. Heat through, ladle into bowls and serve immediately.

Made from cane sugar, the refining process of molasses – when the white sugar is taken away – results in particularly high magnesium which supports the adrenals.

lettuce, pea & tarragon soup

SERVES 4
Prep + cook time: 20 minutes

2 tablespoons butter
8 spring onions, sliced
750 g (1½ lb) frozen peas
1 tablespoon chopped tarragon leaves
1 romaine lettuce, finely shredded
1 litre (1¾ pints) hot vegetable stock (see page 9 for homemade)
2 tablespoons crème fraîche
salt and pepper
tarragon sprigs, to garnish (optional)

Melt the butter in a large saucepan over a medium heat. Add the spring onions and cook, stirring continuously, for 2 minutes.

Stir in the peas, half the tarragon and the lettuce. Cook for 1 minute. Add the stock, bring to the boil, cover and simmer for 5 minutes or until tender.

Add the remaining tarragon and blend until smooth. Season to taste.

Ladle the soup into bowls, swirl the crème fraîche into each bowl and sprinkle with pepper. Garnish with tarragon sprigs, if liked.

For optimum heart health, aim to 'eat the rainbow' every day: a range of fruit and vegetables in different colours will give you maximum nutritional benefit.

spicy fish soup

THE SCIENCE BIT

Studies have shown that people who eat fish, which delivers omega-3 fatty acids, are at lower risk of heart disease and heart attacks.

SERVES 4

Prep + cook time: 20 minutes

2 tablespoons olive oil
1 garlic clove, sliced
1 red chilli, deseeded and finely
   chopped, plus extra sliced chilli to
   serve (optional)
½ teaspoon ground cumin
1 teaspoon paprika
1.5 litres (2½ pints) hot fish stock
   (see page 8 for homemade)
400 g (13 oz) white fish, such as cod
   or haddock, skinned, boned and
   cut into bite-sized chunks
150 g (5 oz) stelline pasta
juice of ½ lemon
salt and pepper
fresh coriander sprigs, to garnish

Heat the oil in a large saucepan, add the garlic and chilli and cook for 30 seconds until beginning to turn golden. Stir in the cumin and paprika, then pour over the stock.

Bring to the boil, then reduce the heat, season, add the fish and simmer for 5 minutes.

Add the pasta and cook for a further 7–10 minutes until the fish and pasta are cooked through.

Ladle into bowls and drizzle over the lemon juice to taste. Serve with sprigs of fresh coriander, and sliced chilli, if liked.

The chilli in this aromatic soup offers even more heart protection. Researchers have found that compounds in chillies can lower blood pressure and reduce blood cholesterol.

red pepper soup

SERVES 4
Prep + cook time: 50 minutes

2 tablespoons olive oil
2 onions, finely chopped
1 garlic clove, crushed
3 red peppers, cored, deseeded and
    roughly chopped
2 courgettes, finely chopped
900 ml (1½ pints) vegetable stock
    (see page 9 for homemade)
    or water
salt and pepper
natural yogurt and chopped chives,
    to garnish

Heat the oil in a large saucepan and gently fry the onions for 5 minutes or until softened and golden brown. Add the garlic and cook gently for 1 minute.

Add the red peppers and half the courgettes and fry for 5–8 minutes or until softened and brown.

Add the stock or water to the pan with salt and pepper and bring to the boil. Reduce the heat, cover the pan and simmer gently for 20 minutes.

When the vegetables are tender, blend the mixture until smooth. Season to taste, reheat and serve topped with the remaining chopped courgette and garnished with yogurt and chopped chives.

This red pepper soup is a top-notch anti-ageing choice. Red peppers are packed with antioxidant vitamins A and C – which combats signs of ageing – and lycopene.

brussels sprout & chestnut soup

SERVES 4
Prep + cook time: 35 minutes

1 tablespoon olive oil
1 onion, finely chopped
1 celery stick, sliced
2 garlic cloves, chopped
500 g (1 lb) Brussels sprouts,
   trimmed and chopped
1.2 litres (2 pints) chicken stock
   (see page 8 for homemade)
300 g (10 oz) canned chestnuts,
   drained and roughly chopped
1 teaspoon celery salt
nutmeg, to taste
salt and pepper
soured cream and chopped chives,
   to garnish

Heat the oil in a large saucepan and sauté the onion, celery and garlic over a medium heat for 5 minutes. Add the chopped Brussels sprouts and sauté for another 5 minutes.

Add the stock, bring to the boil and simmer, covered, for 10 minutes. Add the chestnuts and celery salt and cook for 5 minutes more.

Remove the pan from the heat and let it cool slightly. Blend the soup until smooth. Season with nutmeg and salt and pepper then reheat gently. Serve garnished with a drizzle of soured cream and a few chopped chives.

Chestnuts are rich in mineral salts and a good source of vitamins C, B1 and B2 and, like Brussels sprouts, they are full of fibre.

roasted tomato soup

SERVES 4

Prep + cook time: 25 minutes

1 kg (2 lb) ripe tomatoes, halved
4 garlic cloves, unpeeled
2 tablespoons olive oil
1 onion, chopped
1 carrot, chopped
1 celery stick, sliced
1 red pepper, cored, deseeded and chopped
700 ml (1 pint 3 fl oz) hot vegetable stock (see page 9 for homemade)
salt and pepper
4 tablespoons grated Parmesan cheese, to serve

Place the tomato halves and garlic cloves in a roasting tin. Sprinkle with 1 tablespoon of the olive oil and some pepper and roast in a preheated oven, 200°C (400°F), Gas Mark 6, for 20 minutes.

After 10 minutes, heat the remaining olive oil in a saucepan and sauté the onion, carrot, celery and red pepper over a low heat for 10 minutes.

When the tomatoes are cooked, remove the garlic cloves in their skins and squeeze the garlic flesh into the pan with the sautéed vegetables.

Pour in the roast tomatoes and all the juices along with the stock. Blend the soup until smooth and season to taste.

Reheat the soup if necessary, then serve sprinkled with the grated Parmesan.

kale soup with garlic croûtons

THE SCIENCE BIT

Nutrient-dense kale has a long list of ingredients for all-round health, including vitamins A, B6, C, K, calcium, copper, potassium and antioxidant quercetin.

SERVES 8

Prep + cook time: 1 hour 10 minutes

50 g (2 oz) butter

1 onion, chopped

2 carrots, sliced

500 g (1 lb) kale, tough stalks
    discarded

1.2 litres (2 pints) water

600 ml (1 pint) vegetable stock
    (see page 9 for homemade)

1 tablespoon lemon juice

300 g (10 oz) potatoes, sliced

pinch of grated nutmeg

salt and pepper

2 kale leaves, thinly shredded, to
    garnish

garlic croûtons

90–125 ml (3½–4 fl oz) olive oil

3 garlic cloves, sliced

6–8 slices wholemeal bread, crusts
    removed, cut into 1 cm (½ inch)
    cubes

Melt the butter in a large saucepan, add the onion and cook over a medium heat for 5 minutes or until soft. Stir in the carrots and kale in batches. Cook for 2 minutes until the kale has just wilted.

Pour in the water and stock, then add the lemon juice, potatoes and nutmeg. Season with salt and pepper. Bring to the boil, reduce the heat, cover and simmer for 30–35 minutes until all the vegetables are tender. Add a little water if the soup is too thick.

Make the croûtons while the soup is cooking. Heat the oil in a large frying pan, add the garlic and cook over a medium heat for 1 minute. Add the bread cubes and cook, turning frequently, until golden brown. Remove with a slotted spoon and drain on kitchen paper. Remove and discard the garlic. Add the shredded kale to the pan and cook, stirring constantly, until crispy.

Reheat the soup gently. Ladle into bowls and serve garnished with the croûtons and crispy shredded kale.

spinach & red lentil soup

THE SCIENCE BIT

Crammed with vitamin C, beta-carotene and plenty of antioxidants, spinach is the perfect vegetable for keeping your immune system strong.

SERVES 4
Prep + cook time: 30 minutes

250 g (8 oz) dried red lentils
3 tablespoons sunflower oil
1 large onion, finely chopped
2 garlic cloves, crushed
2.5 cm (1 in) piece fresh root ginger, peeled and grated
1 red chilli, deseeded and chopped, plus extra to garnish (optional)
1 tablespoon medium curry powder
300 ml (½ pint) hot vegetable stock (see page 9 for homemade)
200 g (7 oz) can tomatoes
100 g (3½ oz) baby leaf spinach
25 g (1 oz) chopped coriander leaves, plus extra to garnish
100 ml (3½ fl oz) coconut cream
salt and pepper
4 tablespoons natural yogurt, to serve

Put the lentils into a medium saucepan and cover with 900 ml (1½ pints) cold water. Bring to the boil, skimming off the scum as it rises to the surface, and leave to simmer for 10 minutes until the lentils are tender and just falling apart. Remove from the heat, cover and set aside.

Meanwhile, heat the oil in a large saucepan, add the onion and fry gently for 5 minutes. Add the garlic, ginger and chilli and fry for a further 2 minutes. Stir in the curry powder and ½ teaspoon pepper and cook for a further 2 minutes.

Add the stock, lentils and their cooking liquid, tomatoes, spinach and coriander and season with salt to taste. Cover and simmer for 5 minutes then add the coconut cream. Blend the soup until it is almost smooth.

Ladle the soup into bowls and garnish each with a spoonful of yogurt, the remaining coriander leaves, pepper and finely chopped red chilli, if desired.

seared salmon & wilted spinach soup

THE SCIENCE BIT

This light, yet nutrient-packed broth features salmon which provides vital omega-3 fatty acids plus immune-building spinach and onions.

SERVES 4
Prep + cook time: 20 minutes + standing

750 ml (1¼ pints) fish stock (see page 8 for homemade)
1 teaspoon powdered saffron
1 teaspoon olive oil
2 spring onions, finely sliced
150 ml (5 fl oz) dry white wine
4 × 125 g (4 oz) salmon fillets with skin, cut lengthways into 2–3 strips
200 g (7 oz) baby spinach
salt and pepper
lime wedges and soy sauce, to serve

Bring the stock to the boil in a saucepan and add the saffron. Remove the pan from the heat and leave to infuse for 30 minutes.

Heat the oil in a saucepan over a medium heat, add the spring onions and sauté gently until soft. Add the white wine and boil until reduced by half. Pour in the stock and season with salt and pepper. Remove the pan from the heat.

Brush a griddle pan with a little oil and place over a medium heat for a few minutes. Cook the salmon skin-side down for about 1 minute; turn and cook on the other side for 30–60 seconds. Set aside.

Gently reheat the stock. Add a couple of tablespoons into a pan with the spinach and cook over a high heat for about 1 minute, until the spinach has wilted.

Divide the spinach among 4 bowls. Place the salmon strips in the centre and pour over the hot stock. Serve with lime wedges and soy sauce for drizzling.

tofu & papaya soup

THE SCIENCE BIT

This fragrant soup has an unusual combination of flavours. It is a satisfying meal in a bowl and can be enjoyed hot or cold.

SERVES 4

Prep + cook time: 40 minutes

2 teaspoons olive oil

1 teaspoon sesame oil

1 spring onion, finely chopped

2 garlic cloves, finely chopped

2.5 cm (1 inch) piece fresh root ginger, peeled and finely chopped

1 red chilli, deseeded and finely chopped

1 lemon grass stalk

2 kaffir lime leaves or a strip of lemon rind

juice of 2 limes or 1 tablespoon lemon juice

2 teaspoons ground coriander

750 ml (1¼ pints) chicken or vegetable stock (see pages 8 and 9 for homemade)

500 g (1 lb) fresh papaya, peeled, deseeded and diced

250 g (8 oz) silken or firm tofu, diced

2 tablespoons coconut milk

Heat the olive oil in a large saucepan with the sesame oil and sauté the spring onion, garlic and ginger until soft. Add the chilli and cook for 1 more minute.

Add the lime leaves or lemon rind, lime or lemon juice and ground coriander. Stir in the stock and papaya and simmer for 15 minutes.

Strain the soup through a fine sieve into a clean saucepan. Push it through with a wooden spoon to ensure all the papaya pulp goes through.

Add the tofu and cook for 5 minutes then stir in the coconut milk. If you like, you can serve the soup with a selection of garnishes, such as strips of red pepper, roasted peanuts or cashews, chopped coriander leaves and finely chopped spring onions.

Dubbed the 'fruit of the angels', papaya is chock-full of immune-boosting vitamin C, one large papaya containing up to three times your recommended daily allowance.

quick mushroom & garlic tom yum

THE SCIENCE BIT

A daily helping of garlic is great for health as it contains compounds that help the immune system fight germs.

SERVES 4

Prep + cook time: 15 minutes

1 tablespoon tom yum paste

1 litre (1¾ pints) vegetable stock (see page 9 for homemade)

150 g (5 oz) oyster mushrooms, sliced

200 g (7 oz) closed-cup mushrooms, sliced

100 g (3½ oz) enoki mushrooms (optional)

2 spring onions, thinly sliced

2 garlic cloves, sliced

2.5 cm (1 inch) piece fresh root ginger, peeled and sliced

lime juice, to serve

Place the tom yum paste in a large saucepan with the stock and bring to a simmer. Add the mushrooms, spring onions, garlic and ginger and simmer for 5–6 minutes, so the flavours develop and the mushrooms soften.

Ladle into bowls and serve immediately with a squeeze of lime juice.

Too little sleep and too much stress increase the hormone cortisol which can, over time, suppress immune function so it's important to allow space in your busy life for rest and relaxation.

white bean soup provençal

THE SCIENCE BIT

Beans are ideal for keeping weight in check because they contain tummy-filling fibre, along with protein, another nutrient that curbs cravings.

SERVES 6
Prep + cook time: 35 minutes
 + soaking

3 tablespoons olive oil
2 garlic cloves, crushed
1 small red pepper, cored, deseeded
 and chopped
1 onion, finely chopped
250 g (8 oz) tomatoes, finely
 chopped
1 teaspoon finely chopped thyme
400 g (13 oz) can haricot or
 cannellini beans, rinsed and
 drained
600 ml (1 pint) vegetable stock
 (see page 9 for homemade)
2 tablespoons finely chopped
 flat-leaf parsley
salt and pepper

Heat the oil in a large saucepan, add the garlic, red pepper and onion and cook over a medium heat for 5 minutes or until softened.

Add the tomatoes and thyme and cook for 1 minute. Add the beans and pour in 600 ml (1 pint) water and the stock. Bring to the boil, then reduce the heat, cover and simmer for 15 minutes until the tomatoes are softened.

Sprinkle in the parsley and season with salt and pepper. Serve immediately.

Soup is the dieter's best friend as it stays in your stomach longer so keeps you hunger-free and helps you to stay away from snacks.

chicken, asparagus & tarragon soup

THE SCIENCE BIT

This soup is high in protein, low in carbohydrates, contains only healthy fat and is an excellent choice for anyone following a low-carb diet.

SERVES 4
Prep + cook time: 35 minutes

500 g (1 lb) fresh asparagus
2 tablespoons olive oil
125 g (4 oz) celery, sliced
125 g (4 oz) leeks, sliced
125 g (4 oz) onions, sliced
1.2 litres (2 pints) chicken stock
  (see page 8 for homemade)
200 g (7 oz) silken tofu
300 g (10 oz) cooked chicken, cut
  into bite-sized pieces
1 teaspoon chopped thyme
salt and pepper
2 tablespoons chopped tarragon,
  to garnish

Trim the bottoms of the asparagus stalks where they begin to turn white. Cut off the tips about 3.5 cm (1½ inches) from the top and set aside. Roughly slice the remaining section.

Heat the oil in a large saucepan, add the celery, leeks and onions and fry until soft. Add the stock and bring to the boil. Add the sliced asparagus and simmer for 5 minutes. Remove from the heat, add the silken tofu and blend.

Season with salt and pepper, add the asparagus tips, the chicken pieces and thyme and simmer for 10 minutes. Pour into bowls and sprinkle with the chopped tarragon.

Chicken is a good source of lean protein, especially when the skin is removed, helping you maintain a healthy weight. Protein is a major building block of all muscular tissue in your body.

celeriac, leek & sage soup

SERVES 4
Prep + cook time: 40 minutes

2 large leeks
1 teaspoon extra virgin olive oil
1 large celeriac head, about 400 g
   (13 oz), peeled and roughly cubed
1 onion, roughly chopped
1 garlic clove, finely chopped
1 litre (1¾ pints) chicken or
   vegetable stock (see pages 8 and 9
   for homemade)
1 bay leaf
handful of sage
salt and pepper

Reserve half of 1 leek and cut the remainder into chunks. Heat the oil in a saucepan and sweat the chunks of leek, celeriac, onion and garlic, covered, until soft.

Add the stock, bay leaf and sage and bring to the boil. Cover the pan and simmer for 20 minutes.

Cut the reserved leek into fine strips and blanch for 1 minute in salted water.

Blend the soup until smooth. Season to taste with salt and pepper and serve garnished with the blanched leek strips.

Eating regular meals means you are less likely to be tempted by unhealthy and fattening sugary or high-fat snacks.

fennel soup with olive gremolata

SERVES 4
Prep + cook time: 1 hour

75 ml (3 fl oz) extra-virgin olive oil
3 spring onions, chopped
250 g (8 oz) fennel, trimmed, cored and thinly sliced, reserving any green fronds for the gremolata and chopping them finely
1 potato, diced
finely grated rind and juice of 1 lemon
750 ml (1¼ pints) vegetable stock (see page 9 for homemade)
salt and pepper

gremolata
1 small garlic clove, finely chopped
finely grated rind of 1 lemon
4 tablespoons chopped parsley
16 black olives, pitted and chopped

Heat the oil in a large saucepan, add the spring onions and cook for 5–10 minutes until beginning to soften. Add the fennel, potato and lemon rind and cook for 5 minutes until the fennel begins to soften. Pour in the stock and bring to the boil. Turn down the heat, cover and simmer for about 25 minutes or until the ingredients are tender.

Make the gremolata. Mix together the garlic, lemon rind, chopped fennel fronds and parsley, then stir the chopped olives into the herb mixture. Cover and chill.

Blend the soup and pass it through a sieve to remove any strings of fennel. The soup should not be too thick, so add more stock if necessary. Return it to the rinsed pan. Taste and season well with salt, pepper and plenty of lemon juice.

Ladle the soup into bowls and sprinkle each serving with a portion of the gremolata.

beetroot & apple soup

SERVES 4
Prep + cook time: 20 minutes

1 tablespoon olive oil
1 tablespoon butter
2 Bramley apples, peeled, cored and
   chopped
1 dessert apple, peeled, cored and
   chopped
625 g (1¼ lb) cooked beetroot,
   roughly chopped
2 teaspoons caraway seeds
4–5 fresh thyme sprigs
1.5 litres (2½ pints) vegetable stock
   (see page 9 for homemade)
salt and pepper
crème fraîche, to serve
chopped dill, to garnish

Heat the oil and butter in a large saucepan and fry the apples for 2–3 minutes until golden. Add the cooked beetroot, caraway seeds and thyme and stir-fry for 1–2 minutes. Add the stock, bring to the boil then cook for 10 minutes.

Blend the soup until fairly smooth and season to taste. Ladle into bowls and serve with a swirl of crème fraîche and garnished with chopped dill and pepper.

Cutting down on alcohol and caffeine and avoiding processed food will help to cleanse your body and encourage wellbeing.

carrot, lentil & tahini soup

SERVES 4

Prep + cook time: 55 minutes

2 tablespoons sesame seeds, plus extra for sprinkling
2 tablespoons olive oil
1 onion, chopped
500 g (1 lb) carrots, chopped
1 litre (1¾ pints) vegetable stock (see page 9 for homemade)
2 teaspoons chopped lemon thyme leaves, plus extra for sprinkling
150 g (5 oz) dried green lentils, rinsed and drained
5 tablespoons tahini paste
crème fraîche or Greek yogurt, for topping
salt and pepper

Heat the sesame seeds in a large dry saucepan until lightly toasted. Tip out into a small bowl.

Add the oil to the pan and gently fry the onion and carrots for 10 minutes until softened. Add the stock and thyme and bring to the boil. Reduce the heat, cover and cook very gently for 10 minutes.

Tip in the lentils, cover and cook gently for a further 20 minutes or until the lentils are soft. Remove from the heat, leave to stand for 5 minutes, then stir in the tahini paste. Season to taste with salt and pepper.

Ladle into bowls and top with spoonfuls of crème fraîche or Greek yogurt. Serve sprinkled with extra sesame seeds and thyme.

Don't overload your system. Eat soups, like this lentil-based one, that are full of fibre and stop when you are 80 per cent full.

spinach & watercress soup

THE SCIENCE BIT

Peppery watercress is bursting with vitamins and minerals and has natural diuretic properties to help flush toxins from the body.

SERVES 4
Prep + cook time: 35 minutes

1 tablespoon olive oil
1 onion, finely chopped
325 g (11 oz) potatoes, diced
600 ml (1 pint) chicken or vegetable
   stock (see pages 8 and 9 for
   homemade)
250 g (8 oz) fresh or frozen spinach
75 g (3 oz) watercress
300 ml (½ pint) soya milk
salt
4 tablespoons natural yogurt and
   watercress sprigs, to garnish

Heat the oil in a large saucepan over a medium heat, add the onion and cook for 5–6 minutes until softened. Add the potatoes and stock and simmer for 15 minutes, until the potatoes are cooked.

Add the spinach, watercress and soya milk and simmer for 5 minutes. Remove the pan from the heat and let the soup cool slightly. Season with salt and then blend until smooth.

Ladle the soup into bowls and serve garnished with a tablespoon of yogurt and a watercress sprig.

Spinach helps to clear waste from the body and is an excellent source of antioxidants. It also contains vitamins A, C, calcium, iron and folic acid.

gazpacho

SERVES 4

Prep + cook time: 35 minutes
  + chilling

750 g (1½ lb) ripe tomatoes
1 large fennel bulb
300 ml (½ pint) salted boiling water
¾ teaspoon coriander seeds
½ teaspoon mixed peppercorns
1 tablespoon extra-virgin olive oil
1 large garlic clove, crushed
1 small onion, chopped
1 tablespoon balsamic vinegar
1 tablespoon lemon juice
¾ teaspoon chopped oregano, plus
  extra leaves to garnish
1 teaspoon tomato purée
1 rounded teaspoon rock salt
green olives, finely sliced, to garnish

Put the tomatoes in a large saucepan or heatproof bowl and pour over enough boiling water to cover, then leave for about 1 minute. Drain, skin the tomatoes carefully and roughly chop the flesh.

Trim the green fronds from the fennel and discard. Finely slice the bulb, put in a saucepan and pour over the measurement salted boiling water. Cover and simmer for 10 minutes.

Meanwhile, crush the coriander seeds and peppercorns in a mortar with a pestle. Heat the oil in a large saucepan, add the crushed spices, garlic and onion and cook gently for 5 minutes.

Add the vinegar, lemon juice, tomatoes and chopped oregano to the onion mixture; stir well. Add the fennel and its cooking water, the tomato purée and salt. Bring to a simmer and cook, uncovered, for 10 minutes. Blend to the preferred consistency.; leave to cool. Chill overnight or for at least several hours. Serve garnished with the oregano leaves and olive slices.

SOUPS FOR RECOVERY AND RECUPERATION

introduction

The world over and all through history, food
has been used for healing. As long ago as about
400 BC, the father of medicine, Hippocrates is
reputed to have said 'Let food be thy medicine and
medicine be thy food'. More and more, modern
research is proving that folk remedies really work.
From turmeric to tomatoes and beef to broccoli,
the scientific facts about the health-restoring
components for everyday foods is being revealed.

For instance, as far back as the 12th century physicians
recommended chicken soup to combat a cold. Science has
since found they were right and it can be soothing and
anti-inflammatory for those with colds.

Comforting soup is especially good for aiding recovery from
a range of ailments as it offers an easy way to digest the
essential nutrients that our bodies need. Soup is an excellent
source of hydration, ideal for flushing out the toxins that
result from ill health, and is often more tempting to an
appetite blunted by illness than solid food.

From chicken soup – famously nicknamed 'Jewish penicillin
– for colds to soups targeted at aiding recovery from
hangovers to heartburn, you'll the strengthening soup to
make you feel better in this chapter.

chicken noodle soup

SERVES 4

Prep + cook time: 1 hour + cooling time

2 chicken quarters, about 750 g (1½ lb) in total
1 onion, chopped
4 garlic cloves, chopped
3 slices of fresh root ginger, peeled and bruised
2 litres (3½ pints) cold water
125 g (4 oz) dried egg thread noodles
2 tablespoons light soy sauce
1 red bird's eye chilli, deseeded and sliced
2 spring onions, sliced
2 tablespoons fresh coriander leaves
salt and pepper

Put the chicken quarters, onion, garlic, ginger, measurement water and salt and pepper to taste in a large saucepan. Bring to the boil, then reduce the heat and simmer gently, uncovered, for 30 minutes, skimming off any scum that rises to the surface.

Remove the chicken and strain the stock. Leave to cool, and meanwhile skin the chicken and shred the flesh.

Cook the noodles in boiling water for 6 minutes. Drain well and divide among 4 bowls.

Heat the stock in a saucepan with the soy sauce. Add the chicken and simmer for 5 minutes.

Spoon the stock and chicken over the noodles and sprinkle over the chilli, spring onion slices and coriander leaves. Serve immediately.

Mexican beef chilli soup

THE SCIENCE BIT

Foods rich in zinc, like the steak in this spicy soup, can help improve our immune response to colds and flu.

SERVES 4
Prep + cook time: 20 minutes

2 tablespoons vegetable oil
1 large red pepper, cored, deseeded
   and cut into strips
1 red onion, halved and thinly sliced
1 red chilli, thinly sliced
1½ teaspoons ground cumin
2 tablespoons tomato purée
1 litre (1¾ pints) hot beef stock
   (see page 9 for homemade)
400 g (13 oz) can black beans or
   kidney beans, rinsed and drained
125 g (4 oz) frozen or canned
   sweetcorn, drained if necessary
300 g (10 oz) thick beef steak
2 tablespoons lime juice
coriander leaves, to garnish

Heat 1 tablespoon of the oil in a large saucepan and cook the pepper and onion over a medium-high heat for 4–5 minutes, until lightly coloured. Reduce the heat, add the chilli, cumin and tomato purée and stir for 1 minute.

Add the stock, beans and sweetcorn, then simmer for 5–6 minutes, to allow the flavours to develop.

Meanwhile, heat the remaining tablespoon of oil in a frying pan and cook the steak for 1–2 minutes each side, depending on pinkness desired. Transfer to a plate and leave to rest for 2–3 minutes. Slice the steak into strips, cutting against the grain, and pour any juices from it into the soup.

Ladle the soup into bowls, add the beef and lime juice, garnish with coriander and serve immediately.

celery & horseradish soup

SERVES 4
Prep + cook time: 40 minutes

400 g (13 oz) celery, roughly chopped
1 onion, roughly chopped
4 garlic cloves, crushed
1.2 litres (2 pints) chicken stock (see page 8 for homemade)
2 teaspoons fresh grated horseradish
1 tablespoon white wine vinegar
salt and pepper
chopped parsley, to garnish

Put the celery, onion, garlic and stock into a large saucepan. Bring to the boil then reduce the heat, cover and simmer for 30 minutes.

Blend the soup until smooth, season with salt and pepper and gently reheat.

Add the horseradish and vinegar, stir and serve sprinkled with chopped parsley.

This heart-warming combination will set you on the road to recovery when you have a cold. Using homemade chicken stock would provide extra antibacterial properties.

Haitian chicken & orange consommé

THE SCIENCE BIT

This simple consommé can be served hot or cold and is the perfect drink for when you have a cold.

SERVES 4
Prep + cook time: 40 minutes

1.5 litres (2½ pints) chicken stock (see page 8 for homemade)
500 ml (17 fl oz) freshly squeezed orange juice, strained
2 cloves
2 star anise
1 teaspoon black peppercorns
orange slices, to garnish

Put the chicken stock, orange juice, cloves, star anise and peppercorns into a large saucepan and simmer gently, covered, for 30 minutes.

Strain the soup through a sieve and serve in bowls garnished with thin orange slices. Alternatively, chill and serve cold.

Orange juice provides vitamin C and combines perfectly with the restorative properties of homemade chicken stock. If you feel the need for a little extra nutrition, you can add thin strips of carrot and ginger and some shredded cooked chicken.

oriental soup with egg & greens

THE SCIENCE BIT

Eggs contain a high level of an amino acid called cysteine to mop up toxins from alcohol, plus protein to replenish your body.

SERVES 4
Prep + cook time: 30 minutes

4 spring onions
100 g (3½ oz) pak choi, roughly chopped
2 tablespoons vegetable oil
2.5 cm (1 in) piece fresh root ginger, peeled and finely grated
2 garlic cloves, finely chopped
200 g (7 oz) jasmine rice
100 ml (3½ fl oz) rice wine
2 tablespoons soy sauce
1 teaspoon rice wine vinegar
1 litre (1¾ pints) hot vegetable stock (see page 9 for homemade)
4 eggs
1 tablespoon chilli oil, for drizzling

Finely slice the spring onions, keeping the white and green parts separate. Combine the green bits with the pak choi in a bowl and set aside.

Heat the oil gently in a large saucepan. When hot, add the onion whites, ginger and garlic and stir-fry for 2–3 minutes.

Add the rice, stir, then add the wine and bubble for a minute or so. Add the soy sauce, vinegar and stock and simmer, stirring occasionally, for 10–12 minutes. Then stir in the reserved spring onions and pak choi and cook for a further 2–3 minutes. Meanwhile, poach the eggs.

Ladle the soup into bowls and top each one with a poached egg and drizzle over the chilli oil.

Dehydration is what causes hangovers so drink a large glass of water before you go to bed and alternate alcoholic drinks with water.

borscht

SERVES 6
Prep + cook time: I hour

1 onion, chopped
2 garlic cloves, chopped
500 g (1 lb) beetroot, peeled and
   chopped
1 large cooking apple, peeled and
   chopped
2 celery sticks, chopped
1 red pepper, chopped
125 g (4 oz) mushrooms, chopped
1 tablespoon olive oil
1.8 litres (3 pints) beef stock
   (see page 9 for homemade)
1 teaspoon cumin seeds
pinch of dried thyme
1 large bay leaf
2 tablespoons balsamic vinegar
salt and pepper
200 ml (7 fl oz) soured cream and
   dill sprigs, to garnish

Put the onion, garlic, beetroot, apple, celery, red pepper and mushrooms into a large saucepan with the oil and 3 tablespoons of the stock. Cover and cook gently for 15 minutes, stirring occasionally.

Add the cumin seeds and cook for 1 minute, then add the remaining stock, thyme, bay leaf, balsamic vinegar and salt and pepper to taste. Bring to the boil then reduce the heat and simmer for 30 minutes.

Blend the soup until smooth and creamy, then reheat gently.

Garnish the soup with swirls of soured cream and some dill sprigs before serving.

Beetroot contains phosphorus, sodium, magnesium, calcium, iron and potassium, as well as vitamins A and C and fibre.

tomato & orange soup

The orange juice in this rehydrating soup contains a lot of fructose to help your body get rid of any lingering alcohol.

SERVES 6

Prep + cook time: aout 55 minutes

2 tablespoons olive oil
1 onion, roughly chopped
2 garlic cloves, crushed
2 kg (4 lb) ripe tomatoes, skinned
  and chopped
2 tablespoons tomato purée
450 ml (¾ pint) chicken or
  vegetable stock (see pages 8 and 9
  for homemade)
grated rind of 1 large orange
75 ml (3 fl oz) orange juice
4 basil sprigs
1–2 teaspoons brown sugar
salt and pepper

garnish
2–3 tablespoons finely chopped basil
150 ml (¼ pint) Greek yogurt
6 small basil sprigs
thin strips of orange rind

Heat the oil in a large saucepan and fry the onion and garlic until softened. Add the tomatoes, tomato purée, stock, orange rind and juice and basil. Bring to the boil, then reduce the heat, cover the pan and simmer gently for 20–25 minutes until the vegetables are soft.

Blend the soup until smooth then push through a sieve into the rinsed pan to remove the seeds. Season with salt, pepper and a little sugar.

Return the pan to the heat and bring to the boil, then add a little extra stock or tomato juice if necessary to achieve the desired consistency.

Fold the chopped basil gently into the Greek yogurt. Pour the hot soup into bowls, spoon a little basil yogurt on each one and garnish with small basil sprigs and orange rind.

lemon & spinach soup with white rice

THE SCIENCE BIT

Research suggests an evening meal combining high-GI food, like rice, with protein-rich food, such as eggs, allows us to fall asleep faster.

SERVES 4
Prep + cook time: 40 minutes

2 tablespoons olive or vegetable oil
1 large onion, finely chopped
2 garlic cloves, finely chopped
175 g (6 oz) long-grain white rice, rinsed
1.2 litres (2 pints) clear chicken stock (see page 8 for homemade)
4 tablespoons lemon juice
3 large eggs, beaten
200 g (7 oz) spinach leaves, rinsed and chopped
salt and pepper
chopped parsley and grated Parmesan cheese, to serve

Heat the oil in a large saucepan and cook the onion and garlic gently for 7–8 minutes, until softened. Stir in the rice and cook for 1 minute, then pour in the chicken stock. Simmer gently for 12–15 minutes, until the rice is just tender. Remove from the heat.

Whisk the lemon juice with the beaten eggs and a pinch of salt in a small bowl. Continue whisking while you add a ladleful of hot stock in a slow, steady stream, then whisk the egg mixture into the saucepan of soup.

Return the pan to a very low heat, and continue stirring for 2–3 minutes, until the soup has thickened slightly, taking care not to allow it to boil.

Stir in the chopped spinach and season to taste, then ladle the soup into bowls. Serve scattered with chopped parsley and grated cheese.

broccoli & almond soup

THE SCIENCE BIT

Both almonds and broccoli are excellent sources of magnesium and calcium to promote deeper sleep so you wake refreshed.

SERVES 6
Prep + cook time: 30 minutes

25 g (1 oz) butter
1 onion, roughly chopped
500 g (1 lb) broccoli, cut into florets, stems sliced
40 g (1½ oz) ground almonds
900 ml (1½ pints) chicken or vegetable stock (see pages 8 and 9 for homemade)
300 ml (½ pint) milk
salt and pepper

garnish
15 g (½ oz) butter
6 tablespoons natural yogurt
3 tablespoons flaked almonds

Heat the butter in a large saucepan, add the onion and fry gently for 5 minutes until just beginning to soften. Stir in the broccoli until coated in the butter then add the ground almonds, stock and a little salt and pepper.

Bring to the boil then cover and simmer for 10 minutes until the broccoli is just tender and still bright green. Blend the soup until finely speckled with green and stir in the milk.

Reheat the soup then taste and adjust the seasoning if needed. Heat the 15 g (½ oz) butter in a frying pan, add the almonds and fry for a few minutes, stirring until golden.

Ladle the soup into bowls, drizzle a spoonful of yogurt over each bowl, then sprinkle with almonds.

chamomile, cauliflower & lemon soup

SERVES 4
Prep + cook time: 30 minutes

1.2 litres (2 pints) vegetable stock
   (see page 9 for homemade)
6 chamomile tea bags
1 large cauliflower, trimmed and
   roughly chopped
25 g (1 oz) butter
1 onion, chopped
2 celery sticks, chopped
juice of 1 lemon
salt and pepper
chamomile flowers, chives or lemon
   slices, to garnish

Put the stock and tea bags into a large saucepan and boil for 5 minutes. Remove the tea bags, squeezing the excess liquid into the pan.

Add the cauliflower to the pan, cover and boil for 15 minutes, or until tender.

Melt the butter in a small frying pan and sauté the onion and celery until the onions are translucent. Add to the cauliflower and stock and blend until smooth. Season and add lemon juice to taste.

Gently reheat the soup and ladle into bowls. Serve garnished with chamomile flowers, chopped chives or lemon slices.

Cauliflower belongs to the cruciferous family, which contains two prime disease-fighting ingredients: indole-3-carbinol (or I3C) and the phytonutrient sulforaphane which gets rid of cancerous cells.

Japanese chicken soup

THE SCIENCE BIT

Chicken is high in an amino acid called tryptophan, which has natural sedative qualities to lull you to sleep.

SERVES 6
Prep + cook time: 40 minutes

1 large potato, cut into small chunks
1 daikon or mooli, peeled, shaved lengthways and cut into thin strips
2 onions, finely sliced
750 g (1½ lb) mixed chicken meat (breasts and thigh fillets), cut into bite-sized chunks
500 g (1 lb) firm tofu, cut into bite-sized cubes
200 g (7 oz) shiitake mushrooms, sliced
1 Savoy cabbage, shredded
300 g (10 oz) baby corn, cut into 1 cm (½ inch) chunks
150 ml (¼ pint) soy sauce
1.2 litres (2 pints) chicken stock (see page 8 for homemade)
125 ml (4 fl oz) mirin, dry sherry or sake
salt and pepper

Parboil the potato and daikon strips in boiling water for 10 minutes then drain and reserve.

Put the onions, chicken, tofu, mushrooms, cabbage and corn into a large saucepan with the soy sauce.

Bring the chicken stock to the boil in another pan and add to the chicken mixture. Stir and simmer for about 10 minutes until the chicken is cooked.

Add the potato, daikon and mirin, season with salt and pepper and cook for a few more minutes. Serve steaming hot.

Despite being incredibly healthy and low in fat, this soup is the traditional fare of Sumo wrestlers. Daikon or mooli is a giant white radish which you'll find in Chinese and Asian stores and some large supermarkets.

pesto & lemon soup

SERVES 6

Prep + cook time: 35 minutes

1 tablespoon olive oil

1 onion, finely chopped

2 garlic cloves, finely chopped

2 tomatoes, skinned and chopped

1.2 litres (2 pints) vegetable stock (see page 9 for homemade)

1 tablespoons ready-made pesto, plus extra to serve

grated rind and juice of 1 lemon

100 g (3½ oz) broccoli, cut into small florets, stems sliced

150 g (5 oz) courgettes, diced

100 g (3½ oz) frozen podded soya beans

65 g (2½ oz) small dried pasta shapes

50 g (2 oz) spinach, washed, drained and shredded

salt and pepper

basil leaves, to garnish (optional)

Heat the oil in a saucepan and gently fry the onion for 5 minutes until softened. Add the garlic, tomatoes, stock, pesto, lemon rind and a little salt and pepper and simmer gently for 10 minutes.

Add the broccoli, courgettes, soya beans and pasta shapes and simmer for 6 minutes.

Stir the spinach and lemon juice into the pan and cook for 2 minutes until the spinach has just wilted and the pasta is just tender.

Ladle the soup into bowls, top with extra spoonfuls of pesto and garnish with a few basil leaves, if liked.

A high intake of garlic, onions and leeks, which are all members of the allium family, has been linked to low levels of hip osteoarthritis.

broccoli & black-eyed bean soup

SERVES 4
Prep + cook time: 30 minutes

2 tablespoons olive oil
2 large carrots, peeled and diced
8 spring onions, sliced
1.5 litres (2½ pints) hot vegetable stock (see page 9 for homemade)
300 g (10 oz) purple sprouting broccoli, chopped
400 g (13 oz) can black-eyed beans, rinsed and drained

croûtons
1 slice of crusty wholemeal bread
75 g (3 oz) goats' cheese

Heat 1 tablespoon of the oil in a large saucepan, add the carrots and spring onions and sauté for 2–3 minutes.

Pour in the stock and add the broccoli. Bring to the boil, then reduce the heat and simmer for 10 minutes until the broccoli is tender. Add the black-eyed beans and cook for a further 4–6 minutes until the beans are heated through.

Meanwhile, make the croûtons. Toast the bread under a preheated hot grill for 2–3 minutes on each side, then top with the goats' cheese and grill until the cheese is bubbling. Cut into squares.

Ladle the soup into bowls, then top with the croûtons and sprinkle over the remaining oil.

Changing to a Mediterranean diet – based on fish, olive oil, nuts, beans, fruit and vegetables – has been shown to help ease stiffness in people who have arthritis.

mackerel & cider vichyssoise

SERVES 3–4
Prep + cook time: 45 minutes

625 g (1¼ lb) leeks
50 g (2 oz) butter
625 g (1¼ lb) new potatoes, diced
600 ml (1 pint) strong cider
600 ml (1 pint) fish stock (see page 8 for homemade)
2 teaspoons Dijon mustard
300 g (10 oz) smoked mackerel fillets
5 tablespoons chopped chives
plenty of freshly ground nutmeg
200 g (7 oz) crème fraîche
salt and pepper
chive sprigs, to garnish

Trim the leeks and chop, keeping the white and green parts separate. Melt the butter in a large saucepan and gently fry the white parts and half the green parts for 5 minutes. Add the potatoes, then stir in the cider, stock and mustard and bring almost to the boil. Reduce the heat and cook gently for 20 minutes until the potatoes are soft but still holding their shape.

Flake the smoked mackerel into small pieces, discarding any skin and stray bones. Add to the pan with the chopped chives, nutmeg and remaining green leeks. Simmer gently for 5 minutes.

Stir in half the crème fraîche and season to taste with salt and pepper. Spoon into bowls, top with the remaining crème fraîche and garnish with chive sprigs.

All-round health booster, oily fish is rich in omega-3 fatty acids which help to thin the blood, reduce inflammation and aid brain function.

mushroom ramen

SERVES 4
Prep + cook time: 25 minutes

300 g (10 oz) dried ramen noodles
1.5 litres (2½ pints) vegetable stock
  (see page 9 for homemade)
75 ml (3 fl oz) dark soy sauce
3 tablespoons mirin
350 g (11½ oz) mixed mushrooms,
  trimmed
4 spring onions, thinly sliced
300 g (10 oz) silken tofu, drained
  and diced

Cook the noodles according to the packet instructions. Drain well in a colander, refresh under cold water and set aside.

Combine the stock, soy sauce and mirin in a large saucepan and bring to the boil, then reduce the heat and simmer gently for 5 minutes. Add the mushrooms and simmer gently for a further 5 minutes. Add the spring onions and tofu.

Meanwhile, boil a full kettle of water. Set the noodles, still in the colander, over a sink and pour over the boiling water. Divide the noodles among bowls and pour in the soup. Serve immediately.

This recipe includes mirin. Key to Japanese cuisine, mirin is a sweet rice wine with a light, syrupy texture.

curried mussel soup

SERVES 4

Prep + cook time: 20 minutes

1 tablespoon butter

2 shallots, thinly sliced

2 garlic cloves, crushed

1 teaspoon peeled and finely grated fresh root ginger

2 large red chillies, deseeded and finely diced

1 teaspoon medium curry powder

1 large pinch of saffron threads

100 ml (3½ fl oz) dry white wine

400 ml (14 fl oz) hot vegetable stock (see page 9 for homemade)

1 kg (2¼ lb) live mussels, scrubbed and debearded

200 ml (7 fl oz) double cream

6 tablespoons finely chopped fresh coriander

salt and pepper

Heat the butter in a large wok or frying pan, add the shallots, garlic, ginger, red chillies and curry powder and stir-fry over a high heat for 1 minute. Add the saffron, white wine and stock and bring to the boil, then reduce the heat to medium and cook for 1–2 minutes.

Add the mussels to the pan, discarding any that are cracked or don't shut when tapped, and cover tightly. Increase the heat to high and cook for 2–3 minutes, shaking the pan occasionally, until the mussels have opened. Discard any that remain closed. Remove the mussels with a slotted spoon and set aside.

Pour the cream into the stock mixture and bring back to the boil, then reduce the heat and simmer gently, uncovered, for 5–6 minutes. Return the mussels to the pan, stir in the coriander and season to taste.

Ladle soup into bowls and serve immediately.

jamaican pepperpot soup

THE SCIENCE BIT

Lean meat is a good source of iron and B-complex vitamins. Iron promotes healthy red blood production and prevents anaemia.

SERVES 6

Prep + cook time: 1 hour 30 minutes

1 kg (2 lb) lean stewing beef, cut into cubes
250 g (8 oz) boneless lean pork, cut into cubes
2.5 litres (4 pints) water
24 okra, trimmed and chopped
500 g (1 lb) kale, tough stalks discarded, roughly chopped
2 green peppers, cored, deseeded and chopped
2 spring onions, roughly chopped
sprig of thyme
¼ teaspoon cayenne pepper
500 g (1 lb) yellow yams, peeled and diced
2 small potatoes, peeled and sliced
1 garlic clove, finely chopped
salt

Put the meat and measurement water in a large saucepan. Bring to the boil, then reduce the heat, partially cover and simmer for about 30 minutes.

Add the okra, kale, green peppers and spring onions to the soup with the thyme and cayenne pepper. Partially cover and simmer over a medium heat for 15 minutes.

Tip in the yams, potatoes and garlic and simmer for another 20 minutes or until the yams and potato are tender and the meat is cooked through. Add more water if the soup is too thick. Season with salt before serving.

Vitamin C helps your body absorb iron better, so try to eat foods high in Vitamin C at the same time as those providing iron. Here kale and green peppers provide Vitamin C alongside iron-rich beef.

onion, tomato & chickpea soup

THE SCIENCE BIT

Chickpeas are high in iron and combining them in this soup with vitamin C-packed tomatoes will help your body to absorb it.

SERVES 2

Prep + cook time: I hour
   25 minutes

2 tablespoons olive oil

2 red onions, roughly chopped

2 garlic cloves, finely chopped

2 teaspoons brown sugar

625 g (1¼ lb) tomatoes, skinned if
   liked, roughly chopped

2 teaspoons harissa paste

3 teaspoons tomato purée

400 g (13 oz) can chickpeas, rinsed
   and drained

900 ml (1½ pints) chicken or
   vegetable stock (see pages 8 and 9
   for homemade)

salt and pepper

Heat the oil in a large saucepan, add the onions and fry over a low heat for 10 minutes, stirring occasionally until just beginning to brown around the edges. Stir in the garlic and sugar and cook for 10 more minutes, stirring more frequently as the onions begin to caramelize.

Stir in the tomatoes and harissa paste and fry for 5 minutes. Mix in the tomato purée, chickpeas, stock and salt and pepper and bring to the boil. Cover and simmer for 45 minutes until the tomatoes and onion are very soft. Taste and adjust the seasoning if needed.

Ladle into bowls and serve immediately.

Widely used in North African cooking, fragrant harissa paste is a spicy blend of dried chillies, cumin, garlic, oil and caraway seeds which gives this hearty soup a lift.

ANAEMIA

chunky mushroom soup

THE SCIENCE BIT

Foods that are full of iron, such as mushrooms, fight the tiredness and lethargy caused by iron-deficient anaemia.

SERVES 4
Prep + cook time: 30 minutes

25 g (1 oz) butter
1 large onion, chopped
1 leek, finely sliced
2 garlic cloves, crushed
300 g (10 oz) chestnut mushrooms,
  roughly chopped
2 tablespoons plain flour
500 ml (17 fl oz) vegetable stock
  (see page 9 for homemade)
400 ml (14 fl oz) milk
1 tablespoon finely chopped
  tarragon
salt and pepper

Melt the butter in a large saucepan over a low heat and gently sweat the onion, leek and garlic until they start to soften.

Increase the heat and add the mushrooms to the pan, stirring until well combined. Continue to stir-fry for 2–3 minutes. Stir in the flour and continue to cook for 1 minute.

Remove the pan from the heat and add the stock a little at a time, stirring well between each addition. Once all the stock is added, return the pan to the heat, bring to the boil, reduce the heat and simmer for a few minutes.

Pour in the milk and bring to a simmer. Stir in the chopped tarragon and season to taste.

Ladle the soup into bowls and serve immediately.

smoked haddock & kale soup

SERVES 4
Prep + cook time: 30 minutes

1 tablespoon olive oil
2 shallots, diced
3 garlic cloves, crushed
1 large potato, peeled and diced
350 ml (12 fl oz) soya milk
500 ml (17 fl oz) water
300 g (10 oz) kale, shredded
300 g (10 oz) smoked haddock, skinned and chopped
pepper

Heat the oil in a large saucepan, add the shallots and garlic and cook for 3–4 minutes until softened. Add the potato, milk and measurement water and season with pepper. Bring to the boil, then reduce the heat and simmer for 5–6 minutes.

Stir in the kale and cook for a further 10–12 minutes until the vegetables are tender. Stir in the haddock and simmer for 2 minutes or until cooked through.

Ladle the soup into bowls and serve immediately.

Most of us eat ten times more sodium than we need and cutting down on salt is crucial if you have high blood pressure. Try to avoid cooking with it or adding it to your food at the table.

beetroot & horseradish soup

SERVES 4
Prep + cook time: 50 minutes

1 tablespoon sunflower oil
1 red onion, chopped
1 celery stick, chopped
1 teaspoon chopped thyme
500 g (1 lb) raw beetroot, peeled
  and cut into small chunks
1 tablespoon red wine vinegar
900 ml (1½ pints) hot vegetable
  stock (see page 9 for homemade)
2 tablespoons creamed horseradish
  sauce, plus 2 teaspoons extra
3 tablespoons soured cream or
  crème fraîche
pepper
chopped chives, to garnish

Heat the oil in a large saucepan, add the onion, celery and thyme and cook gently for 3–4 minutes. Add the beetroot and vinegar and cook for 2 minutes.

Pour over the stock, cover and simmer for about 25 minutes until the beetroot is tender. Season to taste with pepper and stir in the horseradish sauce.

Blend the soup until smooth and reheat gently if necessary.

Mix the soured cream or crème fraîche with the remaining horseradish sauce. Spoon on top of the soup and garnish with chopped chives.

Without enough nitric oxide, your arteries can stiffen, raising blood pressure and your risk of heart attack, so aim to eat plenty of nitrite-rich beetroot to build up your body's ability to produce it.

pea, potato & rocket soup

SERVES 4–6
Prep + cook time: 50 minutes

3 tablespoons extra-virgin olive oil, plus extra to serve
1 onion, finely chopped
2 garlic cloves, finely chopped
2 teaspoons chopped thyme
250 g (8 oz) potatoes, chopped
500 g (1 lb) frozen or fresh shelled peas
1 litre (1¾ pints) vegetable stock (see page 9 for homemade)
100 g (3½ oz) rocket leaves, roughly chopped
juice of 1 lemon
pepper

Heat the oil in a large saucepan, add the onion, garlic and thyme and cook over a low heat, stirring frequently, for 5 minutes until the onion is softened. Add the potatoes and cook, stirring frequently, for 5 minutes.

Stir in the peas, stock and season to taste with pepper. Bring to the boil, then reduce the heat, cover and simmer gently for 20 minutes.

Add the rocket and lemon juice and blend until smooth. Adjust the seasoning and heat through. Serve immediately, drizzled with a little extra oil.

The rocket in this soup contains nitrites which are converted to nitric oxide in the body. Nitric oxide has many health benefits, including lowering blood pressure, helping you to sleep and fighting off infections.

parsnip & pumpkin soup

SERVES 4

Prep + cook time: 50 minutes

1 tablespoon olive oil
15 g (½ oz) butter
1 onion, chopped
250 g (8 oz) carrots, chopped
250 g (8 oz) parsnips, chopped
250 g (8 oz) pumpkin, deseeded, skinned and chopped
900 ml (1½ pints) chicken or vegetable stock (see pages 8 and 9 for homemade)
1–2 tablespoons lemon juice
pepper

garnish
1 tablespoon olive oil
1 garlic clove, crushed
1 red chilli, deseeded and finely chopped
3 tablespoons chopped mixed parsley, mint and coriander
generous pinch of ground cumin

Heat the oil and butter in a large saucepan and fry the onion until soft. Add the carrots and parsnips and stir well. Cover the pan and cook over a gentle heat for 5 minutes. Add the pumpkin and cook, covered, for a further 5 minutes.

Pour in the stock and season with pepper. Bring the stock to the boil, cover and simmer for 30 minutes, until all the vegetables are tender.

Blend until smooth; if the soup is too thick, add a little extra water. Reheat the soup and add lemon juice to taste.

Meanwhile, make the garnish. Heat the oil in a small pan, add the garlic, chilli, herbs and cumin and fry for 2 minutes.

Ladle the soup into bowls and spoon a little of the garnish on top.

yogurt, walnut & cucumber soup

THE SCIENCE BIT

Greek yogurt contains probiotics – healthy bacteria that help promote a healthy gut –and is also an excellent source of calcium.

SERVES 4
Prep + time: 15 minutes + soaking and chilling

½ cucumber
25 g (1 oz) walnut pieces
1 garlic clove
4 stems dill
½ slice white bread, torn into pieces
2 tablespoons olive oil
400 g (13 oz) natural yogurt
4 tablespoons cold water
2 teaspoons lemon juice
salt and pepper
olive oil, chopped walnuts and dill sprigs, to garnish

Peel off half the cucumber skin, then roughly chop the cucumber. Put it on to a plate and sprinkle with a little salt. Set aside for 20 minutes.

Rinse the cucumber with cold water and drain well in a sieve. Put the walnuts, garlic, dill, bread and oil into a blender or food processor and whiz until finely chopped. Add the cucumber and yogurt and blend again until the cucumber is finely chopped. Mix in the water, lemon juice and season with salt and pepper to taste. Chill well.

Ladle into glasses. Drizzle the top with a little extra olive oil, sprinkle on a few walnuts and a sprig or two of dill. Serve with strips of toasted pitta bread, if liked.

Refreshing on a summer day, this creamy soup contains walnuts which research has shown could reduce the risk of coronary heart disease if eaten regularly.

mango, lime & ginger soup

SERVES 4
Prep time: 10 minutes

2 large mangoes, peeled and diced
250 g (8 oz) Greek yogurt
1 tablespoon clear honey
juice of 1 lime
500 ml (17 fl oz) unsweetened
   white grape juice
½ teaspoon ground ginger
lime slices, pomegranate seeds or
   edible flowers, to garnish

Put all the ingredients into a food processor or blender and blend until smooth.

Transfer the soup to a bowl, cover and chill. Serve the soup in chilled bowls, and garnish with thin lime slices, pomegranate seeds or edible flowers.

Ginger reduces bloating and its antioxidant qualities will give your whole body a boost, not just your belly.

chilled avocado & palm heart soup

THE SCIENCE BIT

This light, yet satisfying, soup makes a great summer lunch dish that will cool and soothe the digestive tract.

SERVES 4
Prep time: 10 minutes + chilling

3 large avocados, peeled, stoned
   and cut into chunks
juice of 1 lemon
500 g (1 lb) natural yogurt
250 g (8 oz) canned palm hearts
a few drops of Tabasco sauce
500 ml (17 fl oz) vegetable stock
   (see page 9 for homemade)
2 teaspoons chopped coriander
   leaves
salt and pepper
coriander leaves, finely chopped
   tomatoes and spring onions,
    to garnish

Place the avocado chunks in a food processor or blender and sprinkle with the lemon juice.

Add all the remaining ingredients and process until smooth. Cover and chill for at least 1 hour before serving.

Serve in chilled bowls and garnish with coriander leaves, finely chopped tomatoes and spring onions.

Many nutritionists describe avocados as the perfect food because their acid–alkaline content is balanced, making them easily digested. They are high in many essential vitamins and minerals, especially vitamin E which is a powerful antioxidant.

green bean, miso & noodle soup

THE SCIENCE BIT

A fermented paste, the miso in this soup is great for gut health as it is packed with probiotics.

SERVES 2
Prep + cook time: 20 minutes

3 tablespoons brown miso paste
1 litre (1¾ pints) vegetable stock
  (see page 9 for homemade)
25 g (1 oz) fresh root ginger, peeled
  and grated
2 garlic cloves, thinly sliced
1 small hot red chilli, deseeded and
  thinly sliced
100 g (3½ oz) soba, wholemeal or
  plain noodles
1 bunch spring onions, finely
  shredded
100 g (3½ oz) fresh or frozen peas
250 g (8 oz) runner beans, trimmed
  and shredded
3 tablespoons mirin
1 tablespoon sugar
1 tablespoon rice wine vinegar

Blend the miso paste with a dash of the stock in a large saucepan to make a thick, smooth paste. Add a little more stock to thin the paste and then pour in the remainder. Add the ginger, garlic and chilli and bring almost to the boil.

Reduce the heat to a gentle simmer and stir in the noodles, stirring until they have softened into the stock – about 5 minutes.

Add the spring onions, peas, runner beans, mirin, sugar and vinegar and stir well. Cook gently for 1–2 minutes until the vegetables have softened slightly. Ladle into bowls and serve immediately.

Choose ginger to alleviate stomach discomfort. It's a carminative, a substance that promotes the elimination of excessive gas from the digestive system and soothes the intestinal tract.

pea, dill & smoked salmon soup

THE SCIENCE BIT

Foods with a low acid content, such as fish, are good choices if you suffer from heartburn.

SERVES 4
Prep + cook time: 40 minutes

25 g (1 oz) butter
1 large onion, chopped
1 litre (1¾ pints) fish stock
  (see page 8 for homemade)
500 g (1 lb) skinless lightly smoked
  salmon
625 g (1¼ lb) fresh or frozen peas
15 g (½ oz) dill, chopped, plus extra
  for scattering
3 tablespoons crème fraîche, plus
  extra for topping
salt and pepper

Melt the butter in a large saucepan and fry the onion for 5 minutes until softened. Add the stock and bring to a gentle simmer. Lower the fish into the pan and cook gently for 5 minutes until the fish has turned opaque. Lift the fish out with a slotted spoon on to a plate.

Add the peas to the saucepan and bring to the boil. Reduce the heat to its lowest setting, cover and cook for 15 minutes. Ladle about half the soup into a food processor or blender and process until smooth. Return to the pan.

Flake the salmon into small pieces and add to the pan with the dill and crème fraîche. Heat through gently and season to taste with salt and pepper.

Ladle the soup into bowls and spoon a little of the crème fraîche on top of each. Serve scattered with extra dill.

chickpea & parsley soup

THE SCIENCE BIT

For hundreds of years parsley has been used as a medicinal herb for settling the stomach and may help your heartburn.

SERVES 4–6
Prep + cook time: about 2 hours

250 g (8 oz) dried chickpeas, soaked
 overnight
1 small onion, quartered
3 garlic cloves
40 g (1 ½ oz) parsley
2 tablespoons olive oil
1.2 litres (2 pints) vegetable stock
 (see page 9 for homemade)
finely grated rind and juice of
 ½ lemon
salt and pepper

Drain the chickpeas, rinse in cold water and drain again. Put them in a saucepan of fresh water, bring to the boil, boil rapidly for 10 minutes then simmer for 1–1 ½ hours, until just tender.

Put the onion, garlic and parsley in a food processor or blender and blend until finely chopped. Heat the oil in a large saucepan and cook the onion mixture over a low heat until slightly softened.

Add the chickpeas and cook gently for 1–2 minutes. Add the stock, season well with salt and pepper and bring to the boil. Cover and cook for 20 minutes, or until the chickpeas are really tender.

Part blend the soup or mash it with a fork so that it retains plenty of texture. Add the lemon juice and heat through.

Serve the soup topped with grated lemon rind and pepper.

lentil & cumin soup

THE SCIENCE BIT

A healthy well-balanced daily diet, including fresh fruit and veg, whole grains, lentils and fish, can minimize the symptoms of acid reflux.

SERVES 10
Prep + cook time: 50 minutes

3 tablespoons vegetable oil
2 large onions, roughly chopped
4 garlic cloves, crushed
4 teaspoons cumin seeds
500 g (1 lb) dried green or brown lentils, rinsed
1 bay leaf
½ teaspoon dried oregano
3 litres (5 pints) chicken stock (see page 8 for homemade)
150 ml (5 fl oz) soured cream, to garnish

Heat 2 tablespoons of the oil in a large saucepan and sauté the onion, garlic and 3 teaspoons of the cumin seeds for about 5 minutes, letting the onion brown and the cumin roast slightly.

Add the lentils, bay leaf, oregano and stock. Bring to the boil and simmer for about 35 minutes, or until the lentils are soft.

Remove the bay leaf and blend the soup to your preferred texture. You can make it smooth or part blend it if you prefer your soup a little chunkier.

Heat the remaining oil in a small pan and sauté the remaining cumin seeds over a medium heat for about 1 minute, or until they are slightly crisp. Drain on kitchen paper.

Ladle the soup into bowls and garnish with a tablespoon of soured cream and a sprinkling of the roast cumin seeds.

courgette & yellow pepper soup

THE SCIENCE BIT

The yellow pepper in this recipe helps kill harmful bacteria in the body and acts as a digestive aid.

SERVES 4
Prep + cook time: 20 minutes

2 large yellow courgettes, sliced
1 yellow pepper, cored, deseeded
   and chopped
2 garlic cloves, crushed
1 tablespoon chopped thyme leaves
1 litre (1¾ pints) chicken stock
   (see page 8 for homemade)
4 tablespoons low-fat cream cheese
salt and pepper
thyme sprigs, to garnish

Put the courgettes, pepper, garlic and thyme into a large saucepan with the chicken stock and simmer for 10 minutes.

Blend the soup until smooth. Add the cream cheese and blend until the cheese has melted into the soup. Season with salt and pepper. Reheat gently.

Ladle into bowls and garnish with thyme sprigs. This soup is also good chilled.

Peppers stimulate protective mucous membranes in the stomach to ease intestinal inflammation and relieve pain caused by ulcers. They can also buffer pain from other ailments, including arthritis and headaches.

SOUPS FOR THE SOUL AND SPIRIT

introduction

What we eat has a huge impact on how we feel mentally, as well as physically. Recent studies show that a diet high in vegetables, fruit, fish, nuts, whole grains and olive oil could stave off depression. The omega-3 fatty acids found in fish like tuna will fight depression while turkey contains high levels of tryptophan to stimulate the production of serotonin, a natural feel-good chemical produced by our bodies.

Fluctuations in blood sugar lead to swings in mood and energy. Many of the soups in this chapter are based on low-GI pulses and lentils that offer a gradual, steady supply of energy to avoid these ups and downs.

Soup is a go-to option for raising the spirits and providing delicious nutrition all year round: in winter when temperatures plummet a quick bowl of your favourite will work wonders cheering you up. In summer, a chilled soup will refresh and invigorate.

Even making soup can be calming: it's a stress-free way of cooking and the ritual of chopping vegetables and other ingredients and stirring while it bubbles gently on the hob, knowing that you are making a meal your body will benefit from, is soothing.

Alongside eating a balanced diet, it is important to make time for exercise. Scientists have found that regular exercise decreases overall levels of tension, elevates and stabilizes mood, improves sleep and boosts self-esteem.

spiced vegetable & chickpea soup

THE SCIENCE BIT

Escape the whirring loop of stressful thinking by doing something soothingly repetitive like weeding or knitting.

SERVES 4

Prep + cook time: 30 minutes

2 tablespoons olive or vegetable oil
1 onion, chopped
1 green or red pepper, cored, deseeded and chopped
1 aubergine, diced
2 teaspoons peeled and chopped fresh root ginger
1 teaspoon chilli flakes
6 tomatoes, roughly diced
900 ml (1½ pints) hot vegetable stock (see page 9 for homemade)
400 g (13 oz) can chickpeas, rinsed and drained
salt and pepper

Heat the oil in a large saucepan and cook the vegetables and ginger for 7–8 minutes until slightly softened. Add the chilli flakes, tomatoes, hot stock and chickpeas and bring to the boil. Reduce the heat and simmer gently for about 10 minutes until the vegetables are tender.

Blend Blend until smooth, season to taste, then ladle into bowls.

A mug of this soup will provide potassium, vitamin C and vitamin B-6 to support heart health. Chickpeas also contain significant amounts of fibre, which helps lower cholesterol in the blood, thereby decreasing the risk of heart disease.

Thai mixed vegetable soup

SERVES 4
Prep + cook time: 10 minutes

1 tablespoon vegetable oil
1 tablespoon Thai red curry paste
pinch of ground turmeric
150 ml (¼ pint) coconut milk
1 litre (1¾ pints) hot vegetable
  stock (see page 9 for homemade)
1 lemon grass stalk
125 g (4 oz) baby sweetcorn
125 g (4 oz) shiitake mushrooms,
  halved
250 g (8 oz) ready-cooked rice
  noodles
125 g (4 oz) sugar snap peas
50 g (2 oz) bean sprouts
handful of chopped fresh coriander
lime wedges, to serve

Heat the oil in a large, heavy-based saucepan. Add the curry paste and turmeric and cook for 1 minute, then stir in the coconut milk, stock and lemon grass and simmer for 2 minutes.

Add the baby sweetcorn and mushrooms and cook for 2 minutes, then add the noodles and sugar snap peas and cook for a further 3 minutes. Ladle into bowls and top with the bean sprouts. Sprinkle with the coriander leaves and serve with lime wedges.

Making time away from work or family pressures for socializing, exercising or just relaxing in front of your favourite television programme is vital to combat stress.

asparagus & brown rice soup

SERVES 4

Prep + cook time: 40 minutes

1.2 litres (2 pints) chicken or
  vegetable stock (see pages 8 and 9
  for homemade)
2 celery sticks, chopped
½ onion, chopped
1 carrot, grated
1 tablespoon soy sauce
½ teaspoon Tabasco sauce
250 g (8 oz) fresh asparagus, sliced
  into 1 cm (½ inch) pieces
150 g (5 oz) brown rice, cooked
  according to packet instructions
chopped spring onions, to garnish

Put the stock, celery, onion, carrot, soy sauce and Tabasco sauce into a large saucepan and bring to the boil. Reduce the heat and simmer for 15 minutes.

Add the asparagus and the cooked rice and cook for 15 minutes more.

Ladle into bowls and sprinkle with the chopped spring onions.

This soup is a good filler and can be served with a satisfying rough texture or blended to a smooth consistency if you prefer.

turkey meatball & pasta soup

THE SCIENCE BIT

Turkey is rich in protein and in tryptophan which our bodies convert to serotonin which acts to boost happiness.

SERVES 4

Prep + cook time: 30 minutes

500 g (1 lb) turkey mince
50 g (2 oz) fresh white breadcrumbs
25 g (1 oz) Parmesan cheese, grated, plus extra to serve (optional)
2 tablespoons finely chopped flat leaf parsley, plus extra to garnish
1 egg, lightly beaten
1 garlic clove, crushed
2.5 litres (4 pints) hot chicken stock (see page 8 for homemade)
2 large carrots, thinly sliced
175 g (6 oz) farfalline pasta
salt and pepper

Mix together the turkey, breadcrumbs, Parmesan, parsley, egg and garlic in a large bowl and season to taste. Lightly wet your hands, then shape the mixture into small balls about 2 cm (¾ inch) round.

Bring the stock to the boil in a large saucepan, then add the carrots and simmer for 5 minutes.

Drop the turkey meatballs into the stock and cook for 5 minutes. Add the pasta and cook for a further 5–7 minutes or until the meatballs are cooked through. Season to taste.

Ladle into bowls and serve sprinkled with a little Parmesan and chopped parsley, if liked.

Beat the blues with positive thoughts. Studies have shown that thinking and acting in a positive way increases serotonin levels.

roasted butternut, sage & cashew soup

THE SCIENCE BIT

Cashews add an interesting dimension to this soup, plus they're full of selenium. Studies have linked low levels of selenium to depression.

SERVES 4
Prep + cook time: 30 minutes

1 kg (2 lb) butternut squash, peeled, deseeded and chopped into 1 cm (½ inch) chunks
2 tablespoons olive oil
1 tablespoon chopped sage
2 tablespoons pumpkin seeds
1 onion, chopped
1 garlic clove, chopped
½ tablespoon mild curry powder
2 tablespoons cashew nuts
600 ml (1 pint) hot vegetable stock (see page 9 for homemade)
8 tablespoons natural yogurt
salt and pepper

Place the butternut squash in a roasting tin and toss with 1 tablespoon of the oil and the sage. Place in a preheated oven, 220°C (425°F), Gas Mark 7, for 18–20 minutes until tender and golden.

Meanwhile, heat a nonstick frying pan over a medium-low heat and dry-fry the pumpkin seeds for 2–3 minutes, stirring frequently, until golden brown and toasted. Set aside.

Heat the remaining oil in a large saucepan, add the onion and garlic and cook for 4–5 minutes until softened. Stir in the curry powder and cook for a further minute, stirring.

Add the roasted squash, cashews and stock and bring to the boil, then reduce the heat and simmer for 3–4 minutes. Stir in the yogurt. Blend the soup until smooth and season to taste.

Ladle the soup into bowls and serve sprinkled with the toasted pumpkin seeds.

chicken & barley soup

SERVES 8

Prep + cook time: about 4 hours

1 large chicken, weighing 2.5–3 kg
  (5–6 lb), cut into quarters
3 onions
3 large carrots
3 celery sticks
12 garlic cloves
1 lemon, halved
4 bay leaves
600 ml (1 pint) water
250 g (8 oz) pearl barley
1 organic chicken stock cube
4 tablespoons chopped parsley
salt and pepper

Put chicken into a large saucepan with 1 onion,
1 carrot, 1 celery stick, all quartered, the garlic cloves,
and the lemon and bay leaves. Add water to cover
and bring to the boil. Cover with a lid and simmer for
about 1–1½ hours until the meat is tender.

Remove the chicken with a slotted spoon and
place on a large dish to cool. Remove the meat
from the chicken bones, chop it into bite-sized
pieces and reserve. Skim any fat from the surface
of the stock. Put the chicken bones back into the
saucepan, discarding any skin. Add the measurement
water and bring to the boil; reduce the heat and
simmer for 1 hour.

Strain the stock through a sieve, discarding the
vegetables and garlic, and return the liquid to the
pan. Add the pearl barley and cook for 20 minutes
or until done.

Finely chop the remaining vegetables and add to
the stock. Crumble in the stock cube and cook for
about 15 minutes until the vegetables are tender. Add
the chicken and parsley, check seasoning and serve.

DEPRESSION

Sicilian tuna soup

SERVES 4

Prep + cook time: 45 minutes

50 g (2 oz) can anchovies
1 tablespoon olive oil, plus extra
  to drizzle
1 onion, finely chopped
2 garlic cloves, finely chopped
1 courgette, diced
400 g (13 oz) can chopped tomatoes
1 litre (1¾ pints) chicken stock
  (see page 8 for homemade)
2 tablespoons dry sherry
75 g (3 oz) each black and green
  pitted olives, finely sliced
425 g (14 oz) canned cannellini
  beans, rinsed and drained
400 g (13 oz) fresh tuna, cut into
  2.5 cm (1 inch) cubes
juice of 1 lemon
25 g (1 oz) oregano leaves
25 g (1 oz) basil, roughly torn
salt and pepper

Drain the oil from the anchovies into a large saucepan, add the olive oil and warm over a medium heat. Add the onion, garlic and courgette and sauté until the onion is transparent.

Finely chop the anchovies and add to the pan with the chopped tomatoes, stock, sherry and olives. Season with pepper and a little salt if necessary and simmer over a low heat for 15 minutes.

Add the beans and tuna and simmer for a further 15 minutes.

Just before serving, add lemon juice to taste and transfer the soup to a large serving bowl. Sprinkle with the oregano and basil and serve with extra olive oil to drizzle.

With many ingredients that form the basis of the super-healthy Mediterranean diet, this soup offers plenty of omega-3 fatty acids – your brain, heart, circulation and immune system will love it.

lentil, mustard & chickpea soup

SERVES 4

Prep + cook time: 30 minutes

½ teaspoon coconut oil or olive oil

¼ teaspoon mustard seeds

½ teaspoon ground cumin

½ teaspoon turmeric

1 small onion, diced

1.5-cm (¾-inch) piece of fresh root ginger, peeled and finely chopped

1 garlic clove, finely chopped

100 g (3½ oz) red split lentils, rinsed

250 g (8 oz) canned chickpeas, rinsed and drained

900 ml (1½ pints) hot vegetable stock (see page 9 for homemade)

50 g (2 oz) baby spinach leaves

salt and pepper

Heat the oil in a saucepan and add the dry spices. When the mustard seeds start to pop, add the onion, ginger and garlic and cook until the onion softens.

Add the lentils and chickpeas and stir well to coat. Pour in the stock and bring to the boil, then reduce the heat and simmer for 14–16 minutes until the lentils are cooked.

Stir in the spinach until wilted, then season to taste. Ladle the soup into bowls and serve.

This wholesome soup is packed with health-enhancing ingredients, including chickpeas, lentils, spinach, onions, ginger and garlic, to help you feel your best.

raw energy beetroot soup

SERVES 4

Prep + cook time: 20 minutes +
   chilling

1 large beetroot, peeled and cut
   into chunks
1 carrot, sliced
1 small cucumber, peeled and cut
   into chunks
1 red pepper, cored, deseeded and
   roughly chopped
6 tomatoes, skinned, deseeded and
   chopped
1 lemon, peeled, halved and deseeded
1 ripe avocado, peeled, stoned and
   quartered
75 g (3 oz) spinach
75 g (3 oz) alfalfa sprouts, plus extra
   to garnish
25 g (1 oz) dill, chopped
500 ml (17 fl oz) vegetable stock
   (see page 9 for homemade)
salt and pepper

Put the beetroot, carrot, cucumber, red pepper,
tomatoes and lemon in a food processor and blend
until finely chopped. Add the avocado, spinach, alfalfa
sprouts and dill. With the machine running, gradually
add the vegetable stock and process until smooth.

Transfer the soup to a bowl, cover and refrigerate
for at least 2 hours until well chilled. Season to taste
and serve the soup in chilled bowls, garnished with
alfalfa sprouts.

This raw twist on classic borscht is a high-energy
soup that pumps your body full of detoxifying and
immune-boosting nutrients for maximum wellbeing.

fresh herb soup

THE SCIENCE BIT

Combat dehydration with this zingy, fresh broth. Even mild dehydration can affect our mood and sense of emotional balance.

SERVES 4

Prep + cook time: 25 minutes + standing

1 dessertspoon each of the following chopped herbs: flat leaf parsley, curly parsley, chervil, chives, tarragon and marjoram, stalks reserved
750 ml (1¼ pints) chicken or vegetable stock (see pages 8 and 9 for homemade)
50 g (2 oz) butter
1 large potato, diced
1 large leek, finely sliced
squeeze of lemon juice (optional)
salt and pepper

Set the herb leaves aside and put the stalks in a saucepan with the stock. Bring to a simmer and cook for 5 minutes then remove from the heat and leave to infuse for 15 minutes.

Melt the butter in a large saucepan and add the diced potato. Cover and cook over a gentle heat for 8 minutes, moistening the potato with a little stock if it begins to stick. Add the leek and cook for a few minutes more.

Bring the stock back to the boil then strain on to the vegetables. Cook over a medium heat until the vegetables are tender. Add a squeeze of lemon juice, if desired, and season to taste. Just before serving, stir in the chopped herbs.

The green herbs in this tasty broth are packed with phytonutrients to give your immune system a helping hand. You can vary the herbs – try thyme, basil, coriander, dill or rocket.

spring minestrone

SERVES 4–6
Prep + cook time: 1 hour 10 minutes

2 tablespoons olive oil
1 onion, thinly sliced
2 carrots, diced
2 celery sticks, diced
2 garlic cloves
1 potato, peeled and diced
125 g (4 oz) peas or broad beans,
    thawed if frozen
1 courgette, diced
125 g (4 oz) green beans, trimmed,
    cut into 3.5 cm (1½ inch) pieces
125 g (4 oz) plum tomatoes, skinned
    and chopped
1.2 litres (2 pints) vegetable stock
    (see page 9 for homemade)
75 g (3 oz) small pasta shapes
10 basil leaves, torn
salt and pepper
olive oil and grated Parmesan
    cheese, to serve

Heat the oil in a large saucepan over a low heat, add the onion, carrots, celery and garlic and cook, stirring occasionally, for 10 minutes.

Add the potato, peas or broad beans, courgette and green beans and cook, stirring frequently, for 2 minutes. Add the tomatoes, season with salt and pepper and cook for a further 2 minutes.

Pour in the stock and bring to the boil, then reduce the heat and simmer gently for 20 minutes or until all the vegetables are very tender.

Add the pasta and basil to the soup and cook, stirring frequently, until the pasta is al dente. Season with salt and pepper to taste.

Ladle soup into bowls, drizzle with olive oil and sprinkle with the Parmesan before serving.

fragrant soba noodle soup

SERVES 4
Prep + cook time: 20 minutes

1 lemon grass stalk, leaves stripped
1.2 litres (2 pints) clear chicken or
   vegetable stock (see pages 8 and 9
   for homemade)
2.5 cm (1 inch) piece of fresh root
   ginger, peeled and finely chopped
3 lime leaves, thinly sliced
1 small red chilli, deseeded and finely
   sliced (optional)
1 tablespoon fish sauce
250 g (8 oz) buckwheat soba
   noodles
200 g (7 oz) firm tofu, diced
1 spring onion, thinly sliced
2 tablespoons chopped coriander
   leaves

Finely slice the tender hearts of the lemon grass stalks and place in a large saucepan with the chicken stock, ginger, lime leaves, chilli, if using, and fish sauce. Bring to the boil, then reduce the heat to low and simmer gently for 10–12 minutes.

Meanwhile, bring a large saucepan of water to the boil and cook the noodles for 6–7 minutes until tender, or according to the packet instructions. Drain the noodles and divide among 4 bowls.

Scatter the tofu over the noodles and then carefully ladle over the hot, fragrant soup. Scatter over the spring onions and coriander and serve immediately.

Made from pulverized and salted fermented fish, fish sauce adds piquancy to the soup. It has a pungent smell and strong taste so use it sparingly.

minted pea soup

THE SCIENCE BIT

This is a good choice if you have a cold. The menthol in mint acts as a decongestant and to relieve a sore throat.

SERVES 4
Prep + cook time: 30 minutes

1 tablespoon butter
1 onion, finely chopped
1 potato, finely chopped
1 litre (1¾ pints) vegetable stock
  (see page 9 for homemade)
400 g (13 oz) frozen peas
6 tablespoons finely chopped mint
  leaves
salt and pepper
crème fraîche, to serve (optional)

Melt the butter in a large saucepan, add the onion and potato and cook for 5 minutes. Add the stock and bring to the boil, then reduce heat and simmer gently for 10 minutes or until the potato is tender.

Add the peas to the pan and cook for a further 3–4 minutes. Season well with salt and pepper, remove from the heat and stir in the mint. Blend until smooth. Ladle into bowls and top each with a dollop of crème fraîche, if liked.

Pea and mint is a classic combination and a healthy one too: mint promotes good digestion while peas provide a number of key nutrients and contain a polyphenol called coumestrol which has been shown to protect against stomach cancer.

artichoke bisque

THE SCIENCE BIT

Artichokes are a valuable source of vitamins A and C, and are also very effective at detoxifying an overworked liver.

SERVES 4

Prep + cook time: 25 minutes

6 large fresh or frozen artichoke
    hearts, about 500 g (1 lb) in total
25 g (1 oz) butter
1 tablespoon olive oil
3 garlic cloves
900 ml (1½ pints) chicken or
    vegetable stock (see pages 8 and 9
    for homemade)
1 baking potato, diced
salt and pepper
8 small mushrooms, finely sliced,
    to garnish

Thinly slice the artichoke hearts. Melt the butter with the oil in a frying pan, add the garlic and sliced artichokes and sauté gently until the artichokes are tender. Using a slotted spoon, transfer the mixture to a large saucepan, setting the oily pan aside.

Add the stock and potato to the artichoke mixture and bring to the boil. Cover and simmer for about 10–15 minutes, until the artichokes and potatoes are cooked.

Meanwhile, put the mushrooms in the oiled pan and fry over a medium heat, tossing frequently, until they are browned and slightly crispy at the edges.

Blend the soup until smooth and season to taste. Ladle into bowls and garnish with the mushroom slices before serving.

summer vegetable soup

THE SCIENCE BIT

Milder in flavour than onions, leeks are a good base for many soups and are a phenomenal source of vitamins, especially A and K, and a wide range of minerals and antioxidants.

SERVES 4
Prep + cook time: 30 minutes

1 teaspoon olive oil
1 leek, thinly sliced
1 large potato, chopped
450 g (14½ oz) prepared mixed summer vegetables, such as peas, asparagus spears, broad beans and courgettes
2 tablespoons chopped mint, plus extra leaves to garnish
900 ml (1½ pints) vegetable stock (see page 9 for homemade)
2 tablespoons crème fraîche
salt and pepper

Heat the oil in a large saucepan, add the leek and potato and cook for 3–4 minutes until softened.

Add the mixed vegetables to the pan with the mint and stock and bring to the boil. Reduce the heat and simmer for 10 minutes.

Blend the soup until smooth and season to taste with salt and pepper.

Ladle into bowls and serve with the crème fraiche swirled over the top and garnished with extra mint leaves.

Drink plenty of water in warm weather. Add a slice of orange, lime or a chunk of cucumber for a healthy refresher.

Mediterranean tomato soup

SERVES 2

Prep + cook time: 20 minutes

375 g (12 oz) ripe tomatoes, roughly chopped

5 tablespoons olive oil

1 garlic clove, crushed

300 ml (½ pint) hot vegetable stock (see page 9 for homemade)

1 tablespoon tomato purée

½ teaspoon caster sugar

1 teaspoon oregano leaves, plus extra leaves to garnish

1 tablespoon shredded basil leaves

1 ciabatta roll, torn into pieces

2 tablespoons grated Parmesan cheese

salt and pepper

Place the tomatoes in a saucepan with 2 tablespoons of the oil and the garlic. Cook for 3 minutes until softened, then add the stock, tomato purée, sugar, oregano and shredded basil. Bring to the boil, then reduce the heat, cover and simmer for 10 minutes.

Meanwhile, spread the ciabatta pieces over a baking sheet and drizzle over 2 tablespoons of the oil. Toast under a preheated medium grill for a few minutes, turning occasionally, until crisp and golden.

Blend the soup until smooth. Stir in half the Parmesan and season.

Ladle the soup into bowls, drizzle with the remaining oil and top with some of the ciabatta croûtons. Scatter with the remaining Parmesan and a few oregano leaves. Serve with the remaining croûtons.

iced green gazpacho

SERVES 4
Prep time: 20 minutes

2 celery sticks (including leaves)
1 small green pepper, cored and deseeded
1 large cucumber, peeled
3 slices stale white bread, crusts removed
1 fresh green chilli, deseeded
4 garlic cloves
1 teaspoon clear honey
150 g (5 oz) walnuts, lightly toasted
200 g (7 oz) baby spinach
50 g (2 oz) basil leaves
4 tablespoons cider vinegar
250 ml (8 fl oz) extra-virgin olive oil, plus extra for drizzling
6 tablespoons natural yogurt
475 ml (16 fl oz) iced water
handful of ice cubes
salt and pepper
ready-made croutons, to serve

Roughly chop the celery, pepper, cucumber, bread, chilli and garlic.

Place in a blender or food processor and add the honey, walnuts, spinach, basil, vinegar, oil, yogurt, most of the iced water and the ice cubes, and season well. Blend the soup until smooth. Add more iced water, if needed, to achieve the desired consistency. Taste the soup and adjust the seasoning, if necessary.

Serve in chilled bowls and garnish with croutons and a drizzle of olive oil.

Try growing your own herbs to perk up summer soups. It's easy; all you need is a couple of pots or a windowbox and some seeds.

fennel vichyssoise

THE SCIENCE BIT

With a distinctive aniseed flavour, fibre- and vitamin-rich fennel also supports heart health and good digestion.

SERVES 6
Prep + cook time: 50 minutes
+ chilling

25 g (1 oz) butter
1 fennel bulb, about 200–250 g
  (7–8 oz), green feathery tops
  trimmed and reserved, core
  discarded, bulb roughly chopped
4 spring onions, thickly sliced
150 g (5 oz) potato, diced
450 ml (¾ pint) chicken stock
  (see page 8 for homemade)
250 ml (8 fl oz) milk
150 ml (¼ pint) double cream
salt and pepper

Heat the butter in a large saucepan, add the chopped fennel, spring onions and potato, toss in the butter then cover and fry gently for 10 minutes, stirring occasionally until softened but not browned.

Pour in the stock, season and bring to the boil. Cover and simmer for 15 minutes until the vegetables are just tender and still tinged green.

Blend the soup until smooth. Pour the soup through a fine sieve back into the saucepan, then press the coarser pieces of fennel through the sieve using the back of a ladle. Mix in the milk and cream, then taste and adjust the seasoning if needed. Chill well.

Ladle the soup into small bowls or glasses half filled with ice and garnish with the reserved green feathery tops, snipped into small pieces.

potato & smoked garlic soup

SERVES 4
Prep + cook time: 40–50 minutes

50 g (2 oz) butter
1 large onion, sliced
2 smoked garlic cloves, crushed
750 g (1½ lb) floury potatoes,
  peeled and cut into small cubes
1 litre (1¾ pints) vegetable stock
  (see page 9 for homemade)
½ teaspoon smoked sea salt
125 ml (4 fl oz) milk
4 tablespoons chopped fresh herbs,
  such as parsley, thyme and chives,
  plus extra snipped chives to
  garnish
pepper
Greek yogurt, to serve

Melt the butter in a large saucepan, add the onion and smoked garlic and cook over a medium heat for 3–4 minutes until softened. Stir in the potatoes, cover and cook for 5 minutes.

Add the stock and season with the smoked sea salt and pepper. Bring to the boil, then reduce the heat, cover and simmer for 30 minutes until the potatoes are tender.

Blend until smooth, stir in the milk and herbs and reheat the soup gently.

Ladle into bowls and serve with a spoonful of Greek yogurt, garnished with chives and pepper.

Smoked garlic has a mild, sweet taste and will add a delicious note of smokiness to this robust soup.

French onion soup with goats' cheese croutons

SERVES 6
Prep + cook time: 1 hour
   30 minutes

4 tablespoons olive oil
750 g (1½ lb) onions, thinly sliced
2 garlic cloves, crushed
2 tablespoons apple juice
1.2 litres (2 pints) beef stock
   (see page 9 for homemade)
300 ml (10 fl oz) dry white wine
salt and pepper
chives, to garnish

croûtons
1 tablespoon olive oil
1–2 garlic cloves, crushed
3 slices 100% rye bread, cut into
   quarters
250 g (8 oz) goats' cheese

Heat the oil in a large, heavy-based saucepan, add the onions, garlic and apple juice and cook over a high heat for 5–6 minutes, stirring constantly, then turn down the heat to very low and leave the onions to cook for about 20 minutes. The bottom of the pan will turn a deep caramel brown.

Pour the stock and the white wine into the onion mixture and season with salt and pepper. Stir with a wooden spoon, scraping all the juices from the bottom and sides of the pan. Bring to a simmer and leave to cook, uncovered, for about 1 hour.

Meanwhile, make the croûtons. Drizzle the olive oil on a baking tray, add the garlic and spread evenly. Turn the bread in the oil, ensuring both sides are coated. Bake in a preheated oven, 180°F (350°C), Gas Mark 4, for 15 minutes until crispy and crunchy.

Spread the croûtons with a thick layer of goats' cheese and sprinkle with pepper. Heat the grill to high, pour the soup into heatproof bowls and put 2 croûtons into each bowl. Grill until the cheese is bubbling. Sprinkle with chives and serve immediately.

apple & leek soup

SERVES 4
Prep + cook time: 35 minutes

25 g (1 oz) butter
1 tablespoon sunflower oil
450 g (1 lb) leeks, sliced
2 potatoes, peeled and diced
2 dessert apples, peeled, cored
  and diced
150 ml (¼ pint) dry cider
900 ml (1½ pints) vegetable stock
  (see page 9 for homemade)
salt and pepper
grated Gruyère cheese, to serve

Melt the butter with the oil in a large saucepan over a medium heat, add the leeks and cook for 5 minutes until starting to soften.

Stir the potatoes and apples into the pan, cover and cook for a further 5 minutes.

Add the cider and cook, uncovered, until reduced by half. Stir in the stock, cover and simmer for 15 minutes until the potatoes are tender.

Ladle into bowls and serve topped with grated Gruyère cheese.

As the days get shorter and the nights longer, motivation to keep up a health-essential fitness routine can significantly drop. Exercising earlier in the day is one way of making sure you stick with it.

curried parsnip soup

SERVES 4
Prep + cook time: 45–50 minutes

25 g (1 oz) butter
1 tablespoon sunflower oil
1 onion, chopped
2 garlic cloves, crushed
2.5cm (1 inch) piece of fresh root ginger, peeled and chopped
1 tablespoon medium curry powder
1 teaspoon cumin seeds
750 g (1½ lb) parsnips, peeled and chopped
1 litre (1¾ pints) vegetable stock (see page 9 for homemade)
salt and pepper
natural yogurt, chopped fresh coriander, to serve

Melt the butter with the oil in a large saucepan, add the onion, garlic and ginger and cook over a medium heat for 4–5 minutes until softened.

Stir in the curry powder and cumin seeds and cook, stirring constantly, for 2 minutes, then stir in the parsnips, making sure that they are well coated in the spice mixture.

Pour over the stock and bring to the boil, then cover and simmer for 20–25 minutes until the parsnips are tender. Season to taste with salt and pepper.

Blend the soup until smooth, ladle into bowls and serve with dollops of natural yogurt and garnished with the coriander.

You can vary this recipe by using butternut squash instead of the parsnip. Chop up a crisp green apple and add that along with the butternut squash to give an extra tang to the soup.

white bean, bacon & cabbage soup

THE SCIENCE BIT

A Canadian study found that eating one serving of beans daily can reduce your 'bad' (LDL) cholesterol levels by 5 per cent.

SERVES 4
Prep + cook time: 30 minutes

4 tablespoons olive oil
200 g (7 oz) thick-cut bacon, chopped
1 onion, chopped
1 celery stick, sliced
1 carrot, diced
1 litre (1¾ pints) ham stock
1 bay leaf
400 g (13 oz) can cannellini or haricot beans, rinsed and drained
2 tablespoons chopped rosemary
1 small garlic clove, crushed
½ small head of Savoy cabbage, shredded (about 250 g/8 oz prepared weight)
salt and pepper
Parmesan cheese, grated, to serve

Heat 1 tablespoon of the oil in a large saucepan and cook the bacon for 2–3 minutes over a medium-high heat to brown. Add the onion, celery and carrot, reduce the heat slightly, and cook for 5–6 minutes, stirring occasionally, until slightly softened.

Add the stock and bay leaf and bring to the boil. Add the beans and simmer for 10–12 minutes, until the vegetables are almost tender.

Meanwhile, using a small food processor or a pestle and mortar, grind the rosemary with the remaining 3 tablespoons oil, the garlic and a pinch of salt and pepper.

Add the cabbage to the soup and simmer for a further 3–5 minutes, until just tender. Season to taste, then ladle into bowls and serve hot, drizzled with a little rosemary pistou and a sprinkling of Parmesan.

clam & potato chowder

THE SCIENCE BIT

Potassium, found in potatoes and other fruit and vegetables including tomatoes, bananas and sweet potatoes, helps the kidneys work more efficiently.

SERVES 4

Prep + cook time: 45 minutes

1 kg (2 lb) small fresh clams
25 g (1 oz) butter
2 onions, chopped
150 ml (¼ pint) white wine
1.2 litres (2 pints) fish or chicken stock (see page 8 for homemade)
½ teaspoon medium curry paste
¼ teaspoon ground turmeric
500 g (1 lb) floury potatoes, diced
150 g (5 oz) watercress, tough stalks removed
plenty of freshly grated nutmeg
squeeze of lemon juice
salt and pepper

Rinse and check over the clams, discarding any damaged shells or any open ones that don't close when tapped with a knife. Transfer to a bowl. Melt the butter in a large saucepan and gently fry the onions for 6–8 minutes until soft. Add the wine and bring to the boil. Tip in the clams and cover with a lid. Cook for about 5 minutes until the clams have opened, shaking the pan several times.

Once the shells are all open, remove from the heat and tip into a colander set over a bowl to catch the juices. When cool enough to handle, remove the clams from the shells and discard shells. Reserve the clams and tip the cooking juices back into the pan.

Add the stock, curry paste, turmeric and potatoes to the saucepan and bring to the boil. Reduce the heat, cover and simmer for 10–15 minutes until the potatoes are tender.

Return the clams to the pan with the watercress, nutmeg and lemon juice and heat through gently for 2 minutes. Blend the chowder until smooth and season with salt and pepper to taste.

chestnut, rice & pancetta soup

THE SCIENCE BIT

Chestnuts are full of fibre, exceptionally high in vitamin C and contain linoleic acid which is beneficial for cardiovascular health.

SERVES 4
Prep + cook time: 45 minutes

50 g (2 oz) butter
150 g (5 oz) pancetta, diced
1 onion, finely chopped
200 g (7 oz) pack cooked peeled
  chestnuts
150 g (5 oz) risotto rice
500 ml (17 fl oz) chicken stock
  (see page 8 for homemade)
150 ml (¼ pint) milk
salt and pepper

Melt half the butter in a large saucepan and cook the pancetta and onion over a medium heat for 10 minutes.

Cut the chestnuts in half and add to the pan with the rice and stock. Bring to the boil, then reduce the heat and cook gently for 20 minutes or until the rice is tender and most of the liquid has been absorbed.

Heat the milk in a small saucepan until tepid, then stir into the rice with the remaining butter. Season to taste with salt and pepper. Cover and leave to stand for about 5 minutes before serving.

You'll feel better for getting into the fresh air, whatever the weather. Wrap up and head out for a brisk walk to rev up your circulation and keep viruses at bay.

fennel & onion soup with Gruyère toasts

SERVES 4
Prep + cook time: 30 minutes

75 g (3 oz) butter
1 head of fennel, thinly sliced
2 large onions, halved and thinly sliced
2 garlic cloves, roughly chopped
2 teaspoons chopped thyme
1 teaspoon dark soft brown sugar
3 tablespoons brandy or dry sherry
750 ml (1¼ pints) hot beef stock (see page 9 for homemade)
1 teaspoon dark soy sauce (optional)
4 small slices of sourdough bread
100 g (3½ oz) finely grated Gruyère or Emmental cheese
salt and pepper

Melt the butter in a large saucepan over a medium-low heat and cook the fennel, onions, garlic, thyme and sugar for about 20 minutes, stirring occasionally, until soft and slightly caramelized.

Pour in the brandy or sherry and heat until completely evaporated. Add the stock and soy sauce, if using, and bring to the boil, then simmer gently for about 5 minutes. Season to taste.

Meanwhile, top the slices of sourdough with the grated cheese and arrange on a foil-lined grill rack. Place under a preheated medium-hot grill for 2–3 minutes, until the cheese is melting.

Ladle the soup into bowls and top with the Gruyère toasts.

Sourdough is more nutritious and easier to digest than many breads because the lactic acids that ferment the dough make the flour's vitamins and minerals more available to the body.

index

ACKNOWLEDGEMENTS

Thanks to Amanda Cross for the recipes on pages 31, 50, 51, 57, 64, 65, 70, 71, 78, 79, 88, 89, 92, 98, 99, 117, 120, 121, 128, 129, 138, 139, 144, 145, 148, 149, 155, 164.

Photographs
123RF/ABImages 30 left, 32 left, 61 left, 112 right. ahirao 490 left, 170 left. aquariagirl1970 39 left, 55 left, 112 left. Inna Astakhova 16 right, 56 left, 97 left, 98 right, 103 left, 129 right, 150 right. Reinis Bigacs 57 left. Pichest Boonpanchua 19 right, 25 left, 44 right. Sylwia Brataniec 22 right, 141 right, 150 left. byvalet 145 left. cloud7days 35 right. Mykola Davydenko 23 left. Ivan Dzyuba 80–81. Peter Hermes Furion 67 left, 136 left. Yuliya Gontar 132–133. Anton Gorbachev 88 right, 115 right. Andrii Gorulko 40 right, 51 right, 57 right, 97 right, 171 left. indigolotos 64 left. Komanin Intarakamhaeng 91 right. jirkaejc 65 left, 153 right. Sataporn Jiwjalean 103 right. Dmytro Kobeza 12–13. Tatiana Kovalenko 31 right, 127 right, 159 right. Sommai Larkjit 45 left, 49 right, 58, 91 left, 99 right, 108 right, 117 right, 121 right, 123 left, 136 right, 156, 171 right. Dmitry Lobanov 130–131. magone 86 left, 108 left. Markus Mainka 1, 9. Oleksandra Naumenko 82–83. Baiba Oupule 16 left, 29 right, 62 right, 77 right, 127 left, 128 left, 135 left, 138 left, 147 left and right. pinkyone 10–11. Nipaporn Paynacharoen 23 right, 50 right. Suradesh Prapairat 105 right. Penchan Pumpila 15 left, 32 right. Sergey Rasulov 4–5. Roberts Resnais 68 left, 168 left. Volodymyr Shevchuk 71 left. Aliaksei Smalenski 104 left. spafra 73 right, 145 right. somegirl 2–3. tobi 18 right, 46 right, 85 right, 141 left. Valengilda 106 left. Daniel Vincek 19 left, 36 left, 51 left, 69 left, 85 left, 89 left, 99 left, 144 left. Edward Westmacott 44 left. wimi 139 left.
Dreamstime.com/Sergey Galushko 61 right, 67 right, 162 right, 164 right. Goodween 123 120 left. Petr Goskov 121 left. Hamsterman 111 right, 165 right. HandmadePictures 142 right. Ipeema 15 right, 55 right, 86 right, 135 right. Iquaca 74 left, 92 left, 115 left, 148 left. Jcsmilly 88 left, 160 left. Jirkaejc 40 left, 117 left, 167 left. Katerina Kovaleva 26 right, 100 left. Kguzel 98 left. Viktor Kunz 30 right, 31 left, 77 left, 116 right, 148 right, 155 right, 162 left, 170 right. Lrlucik 52 left. Luckypic 36 right, 109 left, 164 left, 173 right. Olga Lupol 138 right. Valentina Razumova 25 right, 35 right, 100 right. Robyn Mackenzie 161 right. Marcomayer 74 right, 79 right, 161 right, 173 right. Marie Maerz 18 left, 167 right. Anna Sedneva 124 right. Pavel Sytsko 20 left, 52 right, 116 left, 123 right, 124 left, 154 left. Pjirawat 50 left, 105 left, 111 left. Radub85 89 right, 93 right, 94 left. Renzzo 39 right, 45 right, 62 left, 64 right, 78 left, 94 right. Olekdandr Rybalka 118 left. Sierpniowka 144 right. Yodsawaj Suriyasirisin 155 left. Danny Smythe 74 right, 106 right, 155 right. Sommai 22 left, 29 left, 43 left, 68 right, 92 right, 93 right, 104 right, 118 right, 120 left, 159 left, 160 right. Tonympix 154 right. Jiri Vaclavek 69 right, 139 right. Yvdavyd 46 left, 168 right.
Octopus Publishing Group/Stephen Conroy 60, 69, 157. Will Heap 21, 28, 34, 38, 42, 53, 63, 66, 75, 87, 90, 107, 110, 169, 172. Lis Parsons 47, 59, 102, 113, 122, 143, 146, 151, 152, 158. Bill Reavell 95. Craig Robertson 48, 54, 140. William Shaw 14, 17, 27, 33, 37, 41, 76, 96, 101, 114, 119, 125, 126, 134, 137, 163, 166. Ian Wallace 24, 72, 84.